THE BRIDGE OVER THE RACIAL DIVIDE

THE AARON WILDAVSKY FORUM
FOR PUBLIC POLICY

Edited by Lee Friedman

This series is to sustain the intellectual excitement that Aaron Wildavsky created for scholars of public policy everywhere. The ideas in each volume are initially presented and discussed at a public lecture and forum held at the University of California.

Aaron Wildavsky, 1930–1993

"Your prolific pen has brought real politics to the study of budgeting, to the analysis of myriad public policies, and to the discovery of the values underlying the political cultures by which peoples live. You have improved every institution with which you have been associated, notably Berkeley's Graduate School of Public Policy, which as Founding Dean you quickened with your restless innovative energy. Advocate of freedom, mentor to policy analysts everywhere."

Yale University, May 1993, from text granting the honorary degree of Doctor of Social Science

RISING

INEQUALITY

AND

COALITION

POLITICS

THE BRIDGE OVER THE RACIAL DIVIDE

WILLIAM JULIUS WILSON

University of California Press
berkeley   los angeles   london

Russell Sage Foundation
new york

University of California Press
Berkeley and Los Angeles, California

University of California Press, Ltd.
London, England

© 1999 by the Regents of the University of California

Library of Congress Cataloging-in-Publication Data

Wilson, William J.
  The bridge over the racial divide : rising inequality and
coalition politics / William Julius Wilson.
    p.   cm. — (Aaron Wildavsky forum for public policy; 2)
  Includes bibliographical references and index.
  ISBN 0-520-22226-1 (alk. paper)
    1. United States—Race relations—Political aspects.
2. Racism—Political aspects—United States. 3. Coalition
(Social sciences). 4. Afro-Americans—Politics and
government. 5. Afro-Americans—Social conditions—
1975– 6. Minorities—United States—Political activity.
7. Minorities—United States—Social conditions. 8. Social
classes—United States—Political activity.   I. Title. II. Series.
  E185.615.W545 1999
    305.8'00973—dc21   99-28663
                                                                   CIP

Manufactured in the United States of America
08 07 06 05 04 03 02 01 00 99 10 9 8 7 6 5 4 3 2 1

The paper used in this publication is both acid-free and
totally chlorine-free (TCF). It meets the minimum
requirements of ANSI/NISO Z39.48-1992 (R 1997)
(*Permanence of Paper*).

In memory of Bayard Rustin, a champion of multiracial political coalitions

CONTENTS

ACKNOWLEDGMENTS

This book is an expansion of the Aaron Wildavsky Memorial Lecture that I delivered in April 1996 at the School for Public Policy, University of California, Berkeley. All of the chapters are original for this book, although a few rewritten paragraphs from *When Work Disappears*, published by Alfred A. Knopf, are integrated into chapters 1, 2, and 4, and parts of a 1997 essay entitled "The New Social Inequality and Affirmative Opportunity" appear in chapters 1 and 4. That essay was published in the Yale University Press volume *The New Majority: Toward a Popular Progressive Politics* (edited by Stanley B. Greenberg and Theda Skocpol).

In the preparation of this book I owe a very special debt to Jennifer Hochschild, Richard Parker, Dalton Conley, and Marshall Ganz, who read the entire first draft of this manuscript and provided detailed comments that led to significant revisions. I am also indebted to Alan Krueger for his very helpful comments on chapters 1 and 2. To Susan Allen, I owe a great deal for her skillful editing of the manuscript to improve its readability for a more general educated audience. To Bruce Rankin, I am grateful for his assistance in developing the figures on growing income and wage inequality. I would also like to thank the students in two of my seminars at Harvard—Race, Class, and Poverty in Urban America and Sociological Perspectives on Racial Inequality—for providing a good sounding board for ideas that eventually found their way into this book. Finally, I would like to thank the Ford Foundation for their support of the Joblessness and Urban Poverty Research Program that I direct at the John F. Kennedy School at Harvard. That support aided the research and travel associated with gathering materials for this book.

INTRODUCTION

In this short book I focus on the rising inequality in American society and on the need for a progressive, multiracial political coalition to combat it. A large, strong, and organized political constituency is essential for the development and implementation of policies that will reverse the trends of the rising inequality and ease the burdens of ordinary families.

Political power is disproportionately concentrated among the elite, most advantaged segments of society. As discussed in chapter 3, the monetary, trade, and tax policies of recent years have arisen from and, in turn, deepened this power imbalance. And, although elite members of society have benefited, ordinary families have fallen further behind. However, as long as middle- and lower-class groups are fragmented along racial lines, they will fail to see how their combined efforts could change the political imbalance and thus promote policies that reflect their interests. Put another way, a vision of American society that highlights racial differences rather than commonalities makes it

difficult for us to see the need and appreciate the potential of
mutual political support across racial lines.

Sadly, in the absence of such a broad-based coalition, America
could develop what the Harvard economist Richard B. Freeman
calls a two-tiered society. He argues that American ideals of political "classlessness" and shared citizenship are threatened by
falling or stagnating real incomes and rising inequality. This
could eventually create a society in which "the successful upper
and upper-middle classes live lives fundamentally different from
the working classes and the poor."[1]

Whereas Americans experienced broadly and rapidly rising
real income from the end of World War II through 1973, after
1973 average wages adjusted for inflation either declined or stagnated for most workers through 1996.[2] Moreover, as seen in figure 1, income inequality that had stabilized through the mid-
1970s began to grow rapidly. Whereas each of the bottom four
quintiles' share of aggregate income declined from 1975 to 1997,
the share of the highest quintile increased significantly, and the
share of the top 5 percent rose considerably above that of the
bottom three-fifths. Indeed, what is particularly striking is that
the top 5 percent's increase in income exceeded the entire income of the bottom 20 percent of families.

These trends are associated with the rate of productivity
growth and the level of skill bias in the economy, but they can
also be related to the strength of what the MIT economist Frank
Levy calls "the nation's equalizing institutions," referring to "the
quality of education, the welfare state, unions, international
trade regulations, and the other political structures that blunt
the most extreme market outcomes and try to insure that most

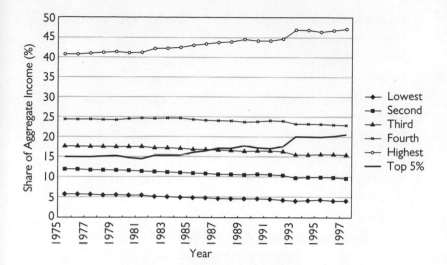

Figure 1.   Share of Aggregate Income Received by Each Fifth
and Top Five Percent of All Families, 1975–1997
Source: Current Population Survey, March 1997.

people benefit from economic growth."[3] As Levy points out,
"We cannot legislate the rate of productivity growth and we cannot legislate the economy's level of skill bias in technological
change and trade. That is why equalizing institutions are important."[4]

There are now signs that this rising inequality has slowed in
the last two years due to the continued strong economic recovery (see pages 61 and 62) and may enter a period of remission as
long as the economy remains strong. However, except for a recent increase in productivity growth, there is little evidence to
suggest that the basic shifts in the economy that have been associated with the rise in inequality are changing.[5] Accordingly, I

see the need for a national multiracial political coalition with a broad-based agenda to strengthen our equalizing institutions. It is essential therefore that the obstacles to multiracial coalition building be removed.

In this book I argue that the racial divide reduces the political effectiveness of ordinary citizens. But I also wish to demonstrate that the likelihood of multiracial political cooperation could increase if we could persuade groups to focus more on the interests that they hold in common. Although there are many similarities in interest among different groups in American society, I believe that the most powerful motivation for group action resides in economic insecurity that results from the decline or stagnation of real incomes linked to changes in the economy, including the global economy.

As I make the case for a multiracial political coalition with a mass-based economic agenda, I also show how such an enterprise can include race-based affirmative action programs that do not create racial friction. This inclusion is an essential aspect of any multiracial effort that seeks to redress current inequalities in race-based employment and education without alienating white supporters.

In laying out the arguments in this book, I am reminded of the words of Ernesto Cortes Jr., head of the Southwest Industrial Areas Foundation—one of the most effective networks of multiracial community organizations in the country. Commenting on Richard Freeman's strategies to combat the rising inequality in American society, Cortes states:

> I hope that progressives in the academic community will
> begin to recognize and appreciate the need for broad-based
> institutional organizing to create the political constituency

necessary to carry [these] strategies forward. . . . Franklin D. Roosevelt is reported to have said about the need for a specific policy initiative, "Okay, you've convinced me. Now go out there and organize and create a constituency to make me do it." I fear that too many progressives are still caught up in the "convincing," when what we need is the constituency— and people who are willing to think hard about how to create, sustain, and energize that constituency.[6]

In this book I examine in theoretical terms how a broad-based political constituency can be created, sustained, and energized. However, I also devote a good deal of space to "convincing"—to making the case for a progressive multiracial political coalition in a society preoccupied with matters that highlight racial differences. Efforts to generate a broad-based political constituency to fight the new inequality will be aided by arguments in support of multiracial coalitions, including arguments that reveal such coalitions' practical and political feasibility.

Although a detailed discussion of the structure of a national multiracial political coalition is beyond the scope and purpose of this short book, I would like to discuss briefly my vision of the essential organizational features of this coalition. I am not speaking here of the formation of a third political party, nor am I referring to a coalition that would be officially aligned with either of the major political parties. Indeed, my idea is that the coalition would be officially bipartisan. The purpose of the coalition would be to put pressure, including voting pressure, on both Democratic and Republican leaders to pursue and adopt policies that reflect the interests of ordinary families. It is true that there are different tensions and currents at work in the Democratic and Republican parties, and many of the progressive issues raised to fight inequality would likely draw more support from Democrats than from Republicans. But if the coalition is perceived to be in a position both to reward and to punish political leaders, members of both parties are likely to take special notice of the coalition's activities.

Specifically, the foundation of the coalition I envision would be organizations committed to fighting social inequality. I have in mind various grassroots community organizations, civil rights groups, women's rights groups, labor unions, and religious organizations, broadly representative of the various racial and ethnic groups and organized in interconnected local, regional, and national networks.* Leaders would be chosen from the national

---

*I see religious organization playing a significant role in this coalition. Some of the strongest advocates for social equality represent religious organizations. The National Council of Churches, representing roughly forty denominations, has an office in Washington, D.C., to lobby for various causes involving justice and equality. Moreover, each of the mainline Protestant churches—Episcopal, Methodist, Presbyterian, American Baptist, United Church of Christ, and Evangelical Lutheran—maintains an office in Washington, D.C., devoted to similar lobbyist activities. As Thad Williamson points out, "With few exceptions, the positions taken by these churches occupy the left edge of the political spectrum. The social statements of these churches reflect concern with both specific issues and, to varying degrees, a sense of deeply-rooted 'structural' injustice in American society. Further, mainline church lobbyists in Washington tend to see themselves as called not so much to represent views of their own members as to act as the voice of 'the poor,' standing in 'prophetic' opposition to the established voice of Washington" (Thad Williamson, "True Prophecy? A Critical Examination of the Sociopolitical Stance of the Mainline Protestant Churches," *Union Seminary Quarterly Review* 51, nos. 1–2 [1997]: 79).

networks and would constitute a coordinating or executive group empowered to represent the interests of the coalition and act on its behalf. Given the potential number and types of groups involved, this coalition could represent a very large constituency. But whatever the main features and structure of the coalition, a case has to be made for why the idea of a national multiracial coalition should be seriously considered. This is the real purpose of my book.

In chapter 1 I argue that our ability to overcome obstacles to the creation of multiracial coalitions will depend on an adequate understanding of the social, economic, and political conditions that cause racial ideology either to flourish or to subside, including the conditions that have contributed to rising inequality in American society. These conditions have also contributed to the rising influence of conservative political messages against minorities, immigrants, and the welfare poor during the first half of the 1990s and especially in 1994 and 1995, before and immediately after the congressional election. The chapter marshals empirical evidence to explicate these conditions and to develop the case for a broader vision of American race relations.

The need for such a vision is made apparent in chapter 2. Perceptions of racial differences obscure the fact that the various racial groups in America suffer from many common problems, including the decreased relative demand for low-skilled labor, the increase in income and wage inequality, and the slow growth of real wages. To illustrate this point, chapter 2 concentrates on the economic changes within the black community. Despite African Americans' understandable focus on racial discrimination, their economic fate is inextricably connected with the structure and functioning of the global economy. I argue that

African Americans perhaps more than any other racial group will benefit from joining forces with others to press for programs of economic reform.

Chapter 3 highlights the fact that rising inequality is not only accompanied by new constraints on the use of federal resources to combat social inequities; it is also occurring at a time when government policies and actions tend to exacerbate rather than alleviate the economic stresses faced by ordinary families. This chapter explains why a national multiracial political coalition is needed to generate programs that improve life for the expanding group of have-nots. It also spells out the conditions that facilitate the formation of such a coalition. Finally, it discusses a current network of community grassroots organizations—the Industrial Areas Foundation (IAF)—that demonstrates how obstacles to sustained interracial cooperation can be overcome.

Chapter 4 addresses an important question that emerges from this discussion of the IAF: whether the divisive issue of affirmative action should be included on the agenda of a national multiracial coalition. Building on the public's perception of affirmative action and highlighting the concepts of affirmative opportunity, flexible merit-based evaluation criteria, and procedural fairness, this chapter shows how affirmative action can be a part of the coalition's agenda without becoming racially divisive. Finally, chapter 5 provides a summary of the preceding chapters and integrates the main arguments on how to bridge the racial divide and how to promote and build support for a progressive multiracial coalition.

I should like to note that throughout the book I use the concept of race in a generic sense, incorporating the concepts of ethnic group and ethnicity. Hence when I refer to multiracial coalitions I mean, in effect, coalitions that include both racial and ethnic groups. As a generic concept, race is, I believe, an important social construct that the public associates with social advantages and disadvantages. It is my view that race should be seen as a social construct because although there may be observed phenotypical differences between groups—that is, visible and immediately identifiable physical characteristics that signal cultural or geographical origin—there is no scientific basis for biological or genetic racial classifications and therefore no evidence that race bestows biological advantages or disadvantages.[7]

By my definition, how one group sees and behaves toward another group determines race. People see and distinguish one another in terms of differences in common ancestry, social and physical environments, and shared communication systems. In some societies these differences are more pronounced than in others. Depending on the degree of intergroup contact, these factors will be associated with differences in tradition, values, belief systems, worldviews, skills, and linguistic patterns.[8] These differences may be enhanced by voluntary or imposed restrictions on actions, and these restrictions can in turn limit opportunities for social and economic advancement. This, then, creates a situation where social factors such as level of economic well-being interact with cultural factors in the formation of observed group traits and characteristics. Thus I emphasize that the concept of race, as used in this book, is a generic social construct that captures group-perceived differences on a range of social and cultural variables.

1

RACIAL ANTAGONISMS
AND THE EXPANDING RANKS
OF THE HAVE-NOTS

A s the new millennium dawns, the movement for racial
equality needs a new political strategy. That strategy must
appeal to America's broad multiracial population while addressing the many problems that afflict disadvantaged minorities and
redressing the legacy of historic racism in America. But in the
last decade, the nation seems to have become more divided on issues pertaining to race. Affirmative action programs are under
heavy assault, and broad public sympathy for those minority individuals who have suffered the most from racial exclusion has
waned.

Today, it seems to me imperative that the concerns of both the
larger American population and the racial minority population
be simultaneously addressed. However, political strategies designed to ease the economic problems that confront the majority
of Americans will not be found until white, black, Latino, Asian,
and Native Americans begin thinking less about their differences

and more about the things they have in common—including common problems, common aspirations, and common hopes.

I believe that proponents of racial equality can pursue policies that unite rather than divide racial groups, thus opening the way for the formation of a multiracial progressive coalition in national politics. This is not a popular view, given the emphasis on racism in the United States and the understandable perceptions that we are "two nations" or an "apartheid society."[1] Let me therefore lay out arguments in support of my position, beginning with a discussion of the challenges to interracial cooperation presented by American racism.

The Challenges of American Racism

Racial tolerance, as expressed in national attitudinal polls, has increased significantly in the last several decades.[2] However, the idea that the federal government "has a special obligation to help improve the living standards of blacks because they have been discriminated against so long" was supported by only one in five whites in 1991.[3]

Several decades ago, efforts to raise the public's awareness and conscience about the plight of African Americans helped enact civil rights legislation and, later, affirmative action programs. By the 1980s, however, African American leaders' assertions that black progress was a "myth" and therefore race-based programs must be strengthened,[4] ironically played into the hands of conservative white critics. Although the leaders' assertion may have increased sympathy among some whites for the plight of black Americans, it also created the erroneous impression that federal antidiscrimination efforts had largely failed. And it overlooked

·the significance of the complex economic changes that have affected the black population since the early 1970s. Perhaps most
pernicious of all, arguments for more and more race-based government programs to help African Americans fed growing concerns, aroused by demagogic messages, that any special effort by
politicians to deal with black Americans' needs and complaints
were coming at the expense of the white majority.[5]*

Meanwhile, from the early 1970s through the first half of the
1990s, national and international economic transformations
placed new stresses on families and communities—stresses
hardly confined to black people. Along with African Americans,
large segments of the white, Latino, Asian, and Native American
populations also experienced growing economic insecurities,
family breakups, and community stresses. Such conditions in-
evitably bred racial and ethnic tensions.

In this social climate, some conservatives have attempted to
unite white Americans around anger at the government and
racial minorities. Their political messages seem plausible to
many white taxpayers, who see themselves as being forced to pay
for programs perceived as benefiting primarily racial minorities.
For example, focus group discussions among blue-collar whites
reveal that they direct some of their anger concerning high taxes
at black welfare recipients.[6] Another study reveals that even
whites who have received public assistance express the same

---

*Perhaps cynicism about such programs was bound to arise: if pres-
ent programs had failed to increase opportunity for racial minorities as
some black leaders proclaimed, who could guarantee that further federal efforts—characterized as costly to the taxpayer and to U.S. business—would be any more successful?

anger. In an interview of working-class men and women in Buf-
falo and Jersey City, Michelle Fine and Lois Weis found that "although many, if not most, of the white men interviewed have
themselves been out of work and have received government
benefits and at times welfare benefits (including food stamps),
they see themselves as deserving of such benefits, in contrast to
blacks whom they see as freeloaders."[7]

Many liberals maintain that such findings reflect underlying
feelings of American racism and that the conservative political
messages during the first half of the 1990s were effective because
they spoke to such feelings. Accordingly, these American liberals
are pessimistic about efforts to bring blacks, whites, and other
racial groups together in a progressive political coalition. They
contend that racist sentiments among many in the society at
large will severely hamper such efforts. This argument is pervasive and widely shared. But it is based on an inadequate understanding of the changing nature, dynamics, and ultimate influence of racism in this society. Let me therefore briefly elaborate
on the changing nature of American racism to bolster the argument that I will soon develop—namely, that racism is not an
overwhelming or insurmountable obstacle to multiracial coalition building.

Racism—a term frequently used imprecisely in discussions of
the conditions of racial minorities in the United States, especially the conditions of African Americans—should be understood as an ideology of racial domination. This ideology features
two things: (1) beliefs that a designated racial group is either biologically or culturally inferior to the dominant group, and (2) the
use of such beliefs to rationalize or prescribe the racial group's

treatment in society and to explain its social position and accomplishments.[8]

Negative feelings about the treatment of a particular racial group can range from the most extreme view that it should be denied the rights and privileges available to the dominant group, to the milder view that the society should make no special efforts to help the group overcome its disadvantages. Regardless of where the view falls on this spectrum, it becomes racist only if it is justified by beliefs that the racial group is biologically or culturally inferior. Accordingly, I identify two types of racism—biological racism and cultural racism. The use of the "justifying" belief in these two types of racism may vary depending upon the treatment that is prescribed for the racial group.

In the United States there is no question that the more categorical forms of racist ideology—in particular, those that represent biological racism—have declined significantly.[9] Unlike in the Jim Crow segregation era from the late 1890s to shortly before the middle of the twentieth century, hardly anyone today is willing to endorse *categorical* beliefs in the biological inferiority of African Americans, including beliefs that blacks should be denied equal rights and privileges because they are biologically inferior or that their relative performance and social position in the United States can be explained in terms of biological capabilities.[10]

But racism is not solely reducible to the belief system of individuals. It may also be embedded in institutional norms and practices. Institutions of society may be considered racist if they function in accord with or convey the idea that ability is associated with race.[11] A clear-cut example comes from the Jim Crow

segregation era. Assumptions that blacks were biologically inferior and therefore unable to learn at the same level or as rapidly
as whites were used to justify school segregation in the South, as
well as the inferior allocation of state resources to African
American schools.

Today, there are virtually no explicit policies to deny blacks or
other minorities equal institutional resources because of their
supposed biological inferiority. Nonetheless, it could be argued
that some institutional arrangements and practices continue to
be guided by *implicit* racist assumptions, especially cultural racist
assumptions. Let me briefly consider this point by focusing on
educational institutions.

In his classic book, *Dark Ghetto*, published in 1965, the fa-
mous African American social psychologist Kenneth B. Clark argues that assumptions of "cultural deprivation" influence decisions on how disadvantaged minority students are to be
educated.[12] Clark points out that among the earliest explanations
of the educational inferiority of black children was that poor average performance reflected inherent racial inferiority. However,
following the publication of the research findings of Otto
Klineberg and other social scientists in the 1930s, scholars seriously reexamined the racial inferiority explanation.

Clark notes that it then became fashionable to attempt to explain the educational progress of African American children in
terms of general environmental conditions—economic and job
discrimination, parental apathy, substandard housing, and poor
nutrition—that depress the ability of these children to learn. He
points out that these environmental explanations come under
the general heading of "cultural deprivation." The cultural deprivation approach, he argues, is seductive.

Indeed, it is presented as a rejection of the inherent racial inferiority theories of the nineteenth and early twentieth centuries. The recent rash of cultural deprivation theories, however, should be subjected to intensive scrutiny to see whether they do, in fact, account for the pervasive academic retardation of Negro children. . . . To what extent are the contemporary social deprivation theories merely substitution notions of environmental immutability fatalism for earlier notions of biologically determined educational unmodifiability? To what extent do these theories obscure more basic reasons for the educational retardation of lower-status children? To what extent do they offer acceptable and desired alibis for educational default: the fact that these children, by and large, do not learn because they are not being taught effectively and they are not being taught because those who are charged with the responsibility of teaching them do not believe that they can learn, do not expect that they can learn, and do not act toward them in ways which help them to learn.[13]

However, the influence of cultural deprivation theories operates in two different ways. First, there are those who believe that minority children who come to school with certain cultural deficits should receive special attention in the classroom so that they can overcome their cultural handicaps and eventually learn and compete at a level equal to those from more privileged backgrounds. Second, there are those who believe that these "cultural deficits" are so ingrained that they are impossible to overcome and that it is unfair to put minority children on the same track or to expect them to reach the same level as white students in the school. This second assumption, which I believe is still accepted among some educators in inner-city schools, is a form of cultural racism. Institutional cultural racism exists when this assumption is embodied in the school's activities and educational arrangements.*

Institutional cultural racism, not only in educational institutions but also in other public and private institutions of American society, impedes the progress of blacks and other minorities and ultimately reinforces individual cultural racist beliefs about their traits and capabilities. As a result, many white Americans are more likely to have an unfavorable impression of African Americans and therefore less likely to join forces with them in a

---

*There may be teachers who do not subscribe to the ideology of cultural racism but who believe that their school is unequipped to provide students from disadvantaged backgrounds with the tools they need to overcome the effects of the environment. Or they may feel that they could bring their students up to the level of other students if they were in a more supportive environment. However, many of their actions and much of their behavior in the classroom, including a feeling of resignation and hopelessness, could be influenced by the implicit cultural racist norms in the school.

And there are others who do not subscribe to the cultural racist ideology but who feel that the students in inner-city schools will not be properly educated until the problems in the larger society are addressed. For example, Jean Anyon argues that to be successful, educational reforms in the public schools have to be part of a larger effort to address the problems of poverty and racial isolation in our inner cities. Anyon calls for a more comprehensive vision of school reform, one that would move beyond attempts simply to change the system of education and instead address more fundamental problems in "the city environment itself," which creates failing schools and destroys the hopes not only of the students and their families but of the teachers and administrators as well (Jean Anyon, *Ghetto Schooling: A Political Economy of Urban Educational Reform* [New York: Teachers College Press, 1997]).

common endeavor. Nonetheless, although it is important to be aware of the challenges presented by institutional cultural racism, its existence hardly supports the view that multiracial coalition building is doomed. The important consideration in coalition building is individual racism rather than institutional racism. In other words, the racial ideologies or stereotypes that individuals endorse could influence their willingness to participate in multiracial organizations, regardless of the level, salience, and type of institutional racism.

Despite the fact that hardly anyone is willing to endorse explicit biological racist arguments, public opinion polls reveal that other forms of individual racial ideology still prevail. In recent years, for example, the General Social Survey, conducted by the National Opinion Research Center of the University of Chicago, changed the questionnaire format it had been using since 1940 to gauge racial stereotypes. Respondents are no longer asked to agree or disagree with "blunt categorical assertions." Instead they are asked to rate blacks, whites, Hispanics, and Asians using bipolar trait rating scales; that is, respondents compare African Americans with other racial groups in terms of work ethic, preference for welfare, and degree of intelligence.[14] These relative judgments reveal that "blacks are rated as less intelligent, more violence prone, lazier, less patriotic, and more likely to prefer living off welfare than whites. Not only are whites rated more favorably than blacks, but on four of the five traits examined [with patriotism the exception] . . . many whites rated the majority of blacks as possessing negative qualities and the majority of whites as possessing positive qualities."[15]

Despite these lingering negative stereotypes, over the past fifty years there has been a steep decline in white support for racial segregation and discrimination. For example, although in 1942 only 42 percent of white Americans supported integrated schooling, by 1993 that figure had skyrocketed to 95 percent. Public opinion polls reveal similar patterns of change during the last five decades in white support for the integration of public accommodations and mass transportation as well as the principle— if not the practice—of integrated residential areas.[16]

However, the virtual disappearance of Jim Crow attitudes in support of racial segregation has not resulted in strong backing for *government programs* to combat discrimination aggressively, to increase integration, to enroll blacks in institutions of higher learning, or to enlarge the proportion of blacks in higher-level occupations. Indeed, as evidenced in the public opinion polls, whites overwhelmingly object to government assistance targeted at blacks: "Support for the principle of equal access to jobs stood at 97 percent in 1972 [the last time this particular question was asked]. Support for federal efforts to prevent job discrimination, however, had only reached 39 percent."[17] Today, whereas eight of every ten African Americans believe that the government is not spending enough to assist black people, only slightly more than three of every ten white Americans feel this way.

The idea that the federal government "has a special obligation to help improve the living standard of blacks" because they "have been discriminated against so long" was supported by only one in five whites in 1991 and has never exceeded more than one in four since 1975. And the lack of white support for this idea is unrelated to background factors such as age and level of education.[18]

How much of this opposition to government programs can be attributed to stereotypes about black cultural traits, such as attitudes, orientations, worldviews, habits, and behavioral styles? In other words, how much of the opposition represents a milder form of cultural racism, the form of racial ideology that Lawrence Bobo and his colleagues have referred to as "laissez-faire" racism, a racism that views blacks as responsible for their own economic predicament and therefore unworthy of special government support.[19] In this connection, James Kluegel's study of trends in white explanations of the black-white economic gap bears eloquent testimony to continued stereotyping: from 1977 to 1989, the most frequently stated reason for the economic gap was the lack of motivation on the part of African Americans.[20]

Conservative supporters of welfare reform implicitly communicated this stereotype in their explanations of the high rates of inner-city joblessness and public assistance and in their opposition to affirmative action programs. When American conservatives explain the high welfare rates of the jobless inner-city poor, they maintain that it reflects the shortcomings of individuals, including their lack of work ethic. Their explanations show little or no appreciation for the harmful behavioral effects that emerge when lack of job opportunities results in persistent joblessness.*

*This is not a problem unique to inner-city blacks. One of the earliest studies to examine the effects of persistent joblessness was conducted for over fifty years in Marienthal, a small industrial community in Austria enduring "a depression that was much worse than anything the United States went through." During the period of research, the entire community of Marienthal was out of work. "One of the main theses of the Marienthal study was that prolonged unemployment leads to a state of apathy in which the victims do not utilize any longer even the few opportunities left to them" (see Marie Jahoda, Paul F. Lazarsfeld, and

In short, although the most virulent forms of individual racial ideology have all but disappeared in American society, a mild form of cultural racist ideology has emerged. And since this ide-

---

Hans Zeisel, *Marienthal: The Sociography of an Unemployed Community* [Chicago: Aldine-Atherton, 1971], vii).

Before this economic depression, when people in the community were working, political organizations were active. People of the town read a lot, "entered eagerly into discussions, and enjoyed organizing a variety of events." The factory was at the center of this lively community. It "was not simply a place of work. It was the center of social life." All of this disappeared when the factory shut down. Describing the situation during their field research in 1930, the authors state:

> Cut off from their work and deprived of contact with the outside
> world, the workers of Marienthal have lost the material and moral
> incentives to make use of their time. Now that they are no longer
> under any pressure, they undertake nothing new and drift gradually
> out of an ordered existence into one that is undisciplined and empty.
> Looking back over any period of this free time, they are unable to
> recall anything worth mentioning.
>
> For hours on end, the men stand around in the street alone or in
> small groups, leaning against the wall of a house or the parapet of
> the bridge. When a vehicle drives through the village they turn their
> heads slightly; several of them smoke pipes. They carry on leisurely
> conversations for which they have unlimited time. Nothing is ur-
> gent anymore; they have forgotten how to hurry. (60)

The idleness and lack of discipline caused by persistent joblessness in Marienthal is similar to the idleness and undisciplined behavior associated with persistent joblessness in today's inner-city neighborhoods. But the common experiences of the long-term unemployed are not mentioned by conservatives when they argue against government programs to aid the jobless poor.

ology supports the idea that African Americans are mainly responsible for their own inferior economic position because of
their cultural traits, many whites conclude that blacks are therefore undeserving of government assistance.[21]

I raise this issue of a persistent subtle racism because I believe
we need a better understanding of majority attitudes toward minority citizens when considering the possibility of multiracial cooperation. And yet I maintain that it would be a mistake to focus
on this new form of racial ideology, however widely endorsed,
when discussing the willingness of Americans to work with other
racial groups in a progressive coalition. Why? Because we need
to consider, for social policy purposes, the extent to which social,
economic, and political factors strengthen or weaken racial ideology and thereby mediate its effects—an argument that I develop in the remaining sections.

Economic Anxiety, Political Rhetoric,
and Ethnic Antagonisms

The degree of support for social policies to address racial inequality is in no small measure related to feelings of economic
anxiety. When affirmative action programs were first discussed
in the 1960s, the economy was expanding and incomes were rising. It was a time of optimism, a time when most Americans believed that their children would have better lives than they had.
During such times a generosity of spirit permits consideration of
sharing an expanding pie.

In the decades immediately after World War II, all income
groups experienced economic advancement, including the poor.
A rising tide did indeed lift all boats. In fact, as revealed in figure 2, between 1947 and 1973 the lowest quintile in family income

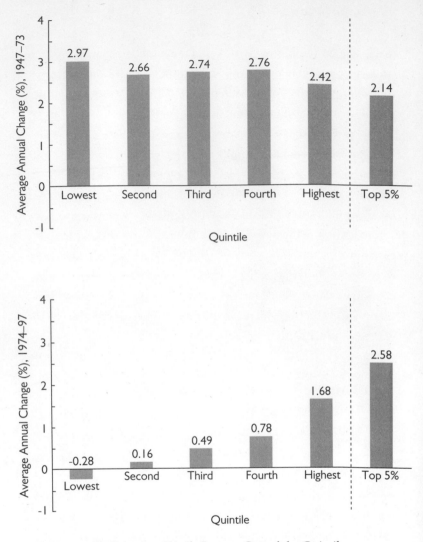

Figure 2. Real Average Family Income Growth by Quintile

Sources: Figures for 1947 to 1973 are from *The Statistical History of the United States, Colonial Times to 1970* and *Money Income of Households, Families, and Persons in the United States, 1992.* Figures for 1974 to 1997 are from the *Current Population Survey,* March 1997. Annual change is calculated using 1997 CPI-U adjusted dollars.

experienced the highest growth in annual income, which meant that the poor were becoming less poor not only in relative terms but in absolute terms as well.[22] This pattern changed, however, in the early 1970s. Economic growth slowed and the distribution of inflation-adjusted income became more unequal. Whereas average income gains from 1974 to 1997 continued for the higher quintiles, especially the top fifth, the lowest quintile experienced annual declines in income during this period, and the second lowest experienced stagnating incomes.

Data on individual wages from 1974 to 1996, based on deciles instead of quintiles (see figure 3), show a pattern in which the bottom of the distribution fell even more. In general, the wages of those at the top continued to climb through this period, while the wages of those below the eighth decile cutoff, the overwhelming majority of workers, declined steadily.

In the 1990s the bottom of the wage distribution stopped its downward plunge, due in large measure to four increases in the minimum wage.[23] On the other hand, the middle of the distribution started to sag (see figure 4). The sagging middle of the distribution, which represents a substantial portion of American workers, "is a major reason for the subdued wage growth in the 1990s."[24]

Since 1979, the median wage for Americans overall, after adjustments are made for inflation, has dipped 10 percent, and the hardest hit have been workers without a college degree—a category that represents three-quarters of the labor force. For example, male high school graduates with five years' work experience have lost an average of almost 30 percent in real wages since 1979. If the economic trends in place before 1973 had continued, argued the economic analyst Jeff Faux in 1997, "a young male

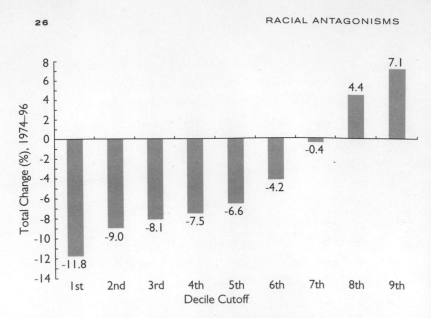

Figure 3.   Real Wage Growth for All Workers, 1974–1996

Source: Monthly Labor Review, December 1997, "Has Wage Inequality Stopped Growing?" Annual data are from the *Current Population Survey,* Outgoing Rotation Group, in 1996 dollars.

high school graduate would be making an annual income of $33,000, as opposed to his current income of $13,000."[25]

Many families were unwilling to accept the lower living standard that their real income implied. Women therefore flooded the labor market, many out of choice, but a sizable percentage out of necessity. "And household debt increased from 58.9% of disposable income in 1973 to an astonishing 94.8% in 1997."[26]

Thus the downward trend in wages during the past two decades has lowered the incomes of the least well-off citizens. Throughout the first half of the 1990s, this trend was accompanied by a growing sense among an increasing number of Ameri-

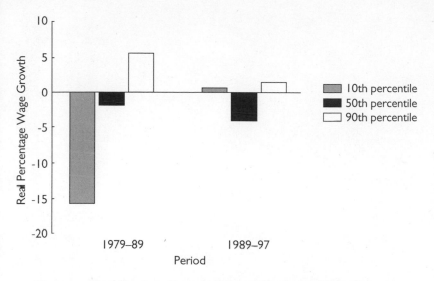

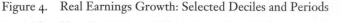

Figure 4.   Real Earnings Growth: Selected Deciles and Periods

Source: Adapted from Alan B. Krueger, "What's Up with Wages?" Mimeo from the Industrial Relations Section, Princeton University, 1997.

cans that their long-term economic prospects are bleaker. And they would not have been reassured to learn that the United States has had the most rapid growth of wage inequality in the Western world. In the 1950s and 1960s the average earnings of college graduates was only about 20 percent higher than that of high school graduates. By 1979 it had increased to 49 percent, and then it rapidly grew to 83 percent by 1992. "Across the board, high-skill groups—college graduates, professionals, managers, older workers—have obtained greater pay increases than low-skill groups. The pay of professional men, for instance, increased by 6 percent while that of laborers fell by 21 percent and that of machine operators fell by 16 percent. The only low-paid group

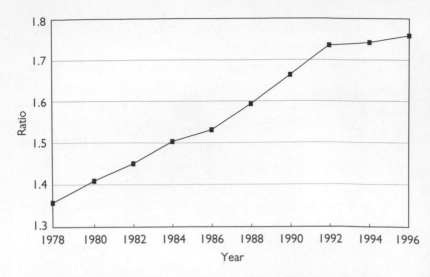

Figure 5.   Payoff to Education: Ratio of Wages of College to High
School Graduates

Source: Adapted from Alan B. Krueger, "What's Up with Wages?" Mimeo from the Industrial
Relations Section, Princeton University, 1997.

whose wages increased were women, whose pay rose relative to
men (though there still remains a male-female pay gap)."[27]

The ratio of earnings of the median college graduate worker
to the median high school graduate worker each year since 1980
is shown in figure 5. Although the ratio may have reached a
plateau in the latter half of the 1990s, in the late 1980s and early
1990s the payoff to education reached record levels. Nearly half
the rise in wage dispersion in the 1980s was linked to education
and experience. "Other breakdowns by skill level (e.g., based on
occupational categories) also show that skilled workers have ex-

perienced an increase in earnings while less-skilled workers have suffered real declines in the last 20 years."[28]

Less-skilled workers have also faced less favorable employment circumstances. Occupations that typically require higher education have had much stronger job growth. For example, between 1984 and 1994, while the fraction of the male population employed increased by 1 percent for college graduates, it fell by 3 percent for high school graduates and 10 percent for high school dropouts. The share of total working hours contributed by college graduates grew from 20 percent of the workforce in 1980 to 26 percent in 1994.[29]

Thus the trends, including the decline of real wages (that is, wages adjusted for inflation), that had begun in early 1973 continued uninterrupted during the first half of the 1990s. Working-class Americans felt economically pinched, barely able to maintain current standards of living even on two incomes. Seven and a half million workers held two or more jobs in 1996, an increase of 65 percent since 1980.[30] Lawrence Mishel and Jared Bernstein of the Economic Policy Institute examined national data on the explanations respondents give for holding more than one job. They reported that "'economic hardship,' the need to meet regular expenses or pay off debts," was the primary reason. Indeed, three-fourths of the roughly 1.17 million additional multiple job holders between 1979 and 1989 said that they were working at more than one job because of economic hardship.[31]

Commenting on this situation, Richard Freeman states:

Falling incomes and rising inequality have occurred despite U.S. success in generating jobs and a huge work effort by

Americans. Since 1974, the U.S. employment/population
ratio has grown from 65 percent to 71 percent while Organization of Economic Cooperation and Development (OECD)
Europe's has fallen from 65 percent to 60 percent. Americans
work considerably more hours and take less vacation than
Europeans; according to the newest OECD data, we even
work more than the Japanese. The experience of prolonged
earnings declines and rising inequality in the context of job
growth and economic expansion is unprecedented in US
economic history.[32]

Many workers were insecure about keeping their jobs. For example, a 1994 nationwide poll revealed that 40 percent of the
workers in America worried that they might be laid off or have
their wages reduced. Many feared that they would never be able
to afford to send their children to college. Many believed that for
all their hard work, their children's lives would be worse than
theirs. For example, a 1995 Harris poll, conducted for *Business
Week*, revealed that only half of all parents expected their children to have a better life than theirs; nearly seven out of ten believed that the American dream has become more difficult to
achieve during the past ten years; and three-quarters felt that the
dream would be even harder to achieve during the next ten
years.[33]

The economic anxiety evident during the first half of the
1990s lingered on through the more robust economic period in
the second half of the 1990s, albeit in a reduced form. Perhaps
this explains why there has been so much worker restraint during
the mid- to late-1990s in the face of a prolonged economic recovery. Since 1993 the U.S. economy has added 18 million jobs.

And the unemployment rate declined to 4.2 percent in March 1999, the lowest in thirty years. Yet prices have not increased much, in part because wages, the main element of costs, have not increased much either.*

Despite high levels of employment and labor shortages in some areas, workers have been surprisingly hesitant to demand higher wages. Few would have predicted that kind of behavior in such a favorable job market. As the MIT economist Paul Krugman recently pointed out, "Apparently the recession and initially jobless recovery left a deep mark on the national psyche."[34] Workers' confidence has been shaken by downsizing and the specter—real or imagined—that many of their jobs can be done for a fraction of their salaries by workers in third-world countries.[35] Indirect evidence of workers' anxiety can be seen in the rate of voluntary resignations. Usually, when unemployment drops, voluntary resignations increase because the favorable job

---

*In addition to the stability of wages, other factors have kept prices from rising significantly. As Louis Uchitelle points out, a rise in the productivity rate since 1997 has also kept prices in check. Workers are producing more goods and services per hour on the job, and the extra revenue from the sales of these "additional goods and services has helped maintain profits without price increases." He also notes that the economic crisis in Asia is helping to hold prices down "in two ways. Asian currencies are falling in relation to the dollar, making American products more expensive in those currencies. To compete, United States exporters are cutting their prices in dollars. Imports from Asia, on the other hand, are less expensive in dollars, also dampening inflation" (Louis Uchitelle, "As Asia Stumbles, U.S. Stays in Economic Stride," *New York Times*, December 7, 1997, p. 4).

market enables those who resign to find new jobs, presumably at higher pay. But during this most recent period of low unemployment, the "quit" rate has decreased.[36]

In a recent survey of a random sample of the American public, 68 percent of the respondents overall, and 72 percent of the non-college graduates surveyed, expressed concern about American companies sending jobs overseas. Commenting on this finding, the Princeton economist Alan Krueger suggests, "The fact that the public is so scared of globalization may mean that wage demands have been moderated as a result."[37]

Workers in the United States feel that they cannot rely on weak unions to bargain effectively for higher wages, and if they lose their jobs they feel compelled to take other employment soon, on whatever terms they can get. "With such a nervous and timid workforce," states Krugman, "the economy can gallop along for a while without setting in motion a wage/price spiral. And so we are left with a paradox: we have more or less full employment only because individual workers do not feel secure in their jobs. . . . The secret of our success is not productivity, but anxiety."[38]

Unfortunately, during periods when people are beset with economic anxiety, they become more receptive to simplistic ideological messages that deflect attention away from the real and complex sources of their problems. These messages increase resentment and often result in public support for mean-spirited initiatives. Candidates for public office and elected officials advance arguments that hinge on the apprehensions of families, including arguments that associate the drop in their living standards with programs for minorities, immigrants, and the welfare poor.[39] During periods of economic duress it is therefore vitally important that leaders channel citizens' frustrations in more positive or constructive directions.

During the first half of the 1990s, a period of heightened economic anxiety as the country was staggering from the effects of the 1990–92 recession, just the opposite frequently occurred. The poisonous rhetoric of certain highly visible spokespersons (such as Pat Buchanan, Louis Farrakhan, Al Sharpton, David Duke, Rush Limbaugh, Governor Pete Wilson, as well as former House Speaker Newt Gingrich and several other House members who framed the 1994 Personal Responsibility Act in the Republican "Contract with America") increased racial tensions and channeled frustrations in ways that divided groups in America. Instead of associating citizens' problems with economic and political changes, these divisive messages encouraged groups to turn on each other—race against race and citizens against immigrants. Perhaps Jeff Faux sums it up best:

> Health care and pension coverage for the typical family has shrunk, full-time permanent jobs are disappearing, and families are putting in longer working hours. As the slowdown in economic growth reduced tax revenues, the public sector's ability to respond to the squeeze on working families has been undercut. Finally, the staggering loss of access to reasonably well-paid jobs for the non-college educated has knocked the rungs out of the ladder of upward mobility, the traditional route through which minorities and immigrants have been integrated into American society. As a result, economic competition among middle- and lower-income workers has intensified, heightening racial and ethnic tensions. And it has fanned the embers of nativist politics while dampening those of the American dream.[40]

Racial Tensions and the
Decline of the Central City

In metropolitan areas, the decline of the central city has aggravated the problems of racial and ethnic tensions. Since 1960, the proportion of whites inside central cities has decreased steadily, while the proportion of minorities has grown. In 1960 the nation's population was evenly divided among cities, suburbs, and rural areas. By 1990 both urban and rural populations had declined, so that suburbs contained nearly half of the nation's population. Urban residents dipped to only 31 percent of the U.S. population by 1990. Although the population of some large cities has been sustained by recent immigration, a study of twelve central cities found that only three had attracted more immigrants than did their suburbs. The study also found that "the higher the level of household income, the more likely an immigrant household would settle in the suburbs."[41] Beginning in the mid-1970s, the employment balance between central cities and suburbs shifted markedly to the suburbs. Manufacturing is now over 70 percent suburban; wholesale and retail trade is just under 70 percent. Since 1980, over two-thirds of employment growth has occurred outside the central city. And during the economic recovery period of 1991 to 1994, a period during which nearly six million jobs were created nationally, cities of all sizes lost significant ground to suburbs in job growth (see figure 6). Job growth in the ten largest cities declined by almost 3 percent while it increased by more than 9 percent in the surrounding suburbs.

If declining opportunities for employment in the central cities have been notable, the growth of concentrated poverty has been even more dramatic. High-poverty neighborhoods, in which at

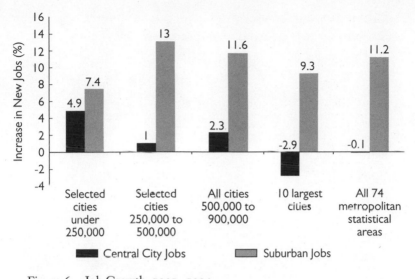

Figure 6.   Job Growth, 1991–1994

Source: U.S. Department of Housing and Urban Development, May 27, 1997.

least 40 percent of the residents live in poverty, have grown at an alarming rate. Since 1970, the population in high-poverty met- ropolitan neighborhoods—be they black ghettos, Latino barrios, or white slums—grew by 92 percent. Eight million people now live in these high-poverty metropolitan areas, and nearly all the growth in poverty-impaired areas has occurred in central cities and inner-ring suburbs, which suffer from middle-class flight and commercial decay.[42]

It is important to note that the increase in the number of res- idents in high-poverty neighborhoods—and especially in black ghettos, which account for roughly half of all high-poverty areas—is strongly related to the geographical spread of these neighborhoods. In other words, the number of persons living in ghettos grew not because more people moved into them, "but because the poverty spread to more and more neighborhoods."[43]

The exodus of the nonpoor from mixed income areas was a major factor in the spread of ghettos during the 1970s. Since 1980, the areas classified as ghetto census tracts by the U.S. Census have increased in a substantial majority of the country's central city areas, including those census tracts with fewer people living in them. Nine census tracts were newly classified as "ghetto" in Philadelphia even though this city experienced one of the largest declines in the proportion of people living in ghetto tracts. In a number of other cities, including Baltimore, Boston, Chicago, and the District of Columbia, a smaller percentage of poor blacks live in a larger number of ghetto census tracts. The geographic spread of poverty neighborhoods has a powerful impact on the way others perceive the magnitude of the problems of urban privation and decay. As more and more city neighborhoods become classified as "dangerous" by middle- and working-class citizens, the ghetto tracts fall into a seemingly irreversible isolation. How far out of the way will citizens drive to avoid these areas?[44]

The demographic changes in American cities are related to the cities' declining influence in the determination of domestic policy, and these changes contributed to the rise of the New Federalism. Beginning in 1980, the federal government drastically decreased its support for basic urban programs. The Reagan and Bush administrations—proponents of the New Federalism, which insisted on localized responses to social problems—sharply cut federal spending on direct aid to cities, including general revenue sharing, urban mass transit, public service jobs and job training, compensatory education, social service block grants, local public works, economic development assistance, and urban development action grants.[45] In 1980 the federal contribution to city budgets was 18 percent; by 1990 it had dropped to 6.4 percent.

In general, state governments have not compensated cities for these cuts in direct federal aid. City governments have therefore had to rely increasingly on local taxes. But as economic activity and wealth shifted to the suburbs, incomes in cities declined. Note that in 1973 average per capita income between cities and suburbs was nearly equal; by 1989 the average city income had dipped 16 percent below that of the suburbs.[46] With a declining tax base and loss of federal funds, many city governments experienced difficulty in raising sufficient revenue to pay for basic services. Cities often avoided bankruptcy by cutting services. For example, many public schools were unable to upgrade their facilities, attract talented administrators and teachers, or even purchase new textbooks throughout the 1980s.[47]

As the social and political forces turned against the cities, businesses became more reluctant to invest in urban areas. All of these social and economic changes have resulted in a decline in the quality of urban life. Pollution has spread and services have fallen away. And although violent crime and drug use and abuse have declined in the last few years, the city is still perceived by many as a dangerous place to live.[48] For all these reasons, many urban residents—especially those in the nation's largest cities—moved, if they had the choice, to outlying sections of metropolitan areas.

Thus, to many in the dominant white population, minorities symbolize the ugly urban scene left behind. Today, the divide between the suburbs and the city is in many respects a racial divide.

Across the nation in 1990, three-quarters of the dominant white population lived in suburban and rural areas, while African Americans and Latinos resided largely in urban areas.[49]

But although there is a clear racial divide between the central city and the suburbs, racial tensions in metropolitan areas continue to be concentrated in the central city. They affect relations and patterns of interaction among blacks, other minorities, and urban whites—especially the lower-income whites—who remain.

It will be difficult to address growing racial tensions in U.S. cities unless we tackle the problems of limited revenue and inadequate social services and the gradual disappearance of work in certain neighborhoods. Despite the improvement in the financial health of many urban areas in the last few years as a result of the prolonged economic recovery, the city has become for many a less desirable place in which to live, and the demographic, economic, and social gaps between the city and suburbs continue to grow. Those who remain in the city compete, often along racial lines, for limited resources, including the remaining decent schools, housing, and neighborhoods. All of these factors aggravate intergroup relations and elevate racial tensions. Racist ideology—in particular, the cultural racist ideology that associates the decline of the central city with minorities' ways of life—blossoms in such a climate.

We must understand that racial antagonisms are products of situations—economic situations, political situations, and social situations. Average citizens do not fully understand the complex forces that have increased their economic woes—the slowing of economic growth and the declines in annual real family income;

changes in the global economy and the rise in wage dispersion, industry relocation, and urban employment opportunities; the New Federalism and the decline of the central city. They are looking for answers as they cope with their own anxieties.

The answers that have recently proved to be the most powerful and persuasive to the general public have come not from progressives, who are more likely to associate economic and social problems with the complex changes of the late twentieth century. Rather, they have come from conservative spokespersons who utter effective, often mean-spirited sound bites that deflect attention from the real sources of our problems.

Sadly these sound bites include messages directed against minorities and affirmative action, immigrants, and welfare recipients. The effectiveness of these messages was demonstrated in the months leading up to and following the congressional election of 1994, when conservative Republicans gained control of the U.S. Congress. However, since 1996 the frequency and intensity of these messages have noticeably decreased. I think that we can thank continued improvement in the economy for that. Ordinary Americans are still economically anxious and continue to be worried about their future, and with good reason, but public opinion polls reveal that they are more satisfied today than they were in 1994, when the Republicans took over Congress, and in 1995, when conservative political leaders perceived that their pronouncements about the adverse effects of affirmative action, welfare, and immigration would resonate with the general population. I believe that now is the time for proponents of multiracial coalitions to build on this shift in the public's mood.

Toward an Effective Multiracial
Political Coalition

Despite the persistence of cultural racism, if we develop a new
public dialogue on how our problems should be defined and how
they should be addressed, we can create a climate in the United
States that bridges the divide among groups and lays the foundation for multiracial political cooperation. It is important to appreciate, first of all, that the poor and the working classes of all
racial groups struggle to make ends meet, and that even the middle class has experienced a decline in its living standard. And unlike the top 20 percent of the U.S. population, these groups are
indeed struggling: "virtually all of the past decade's economic
growth has gone to the upper 5 percent of families. Since the
early 1970s, while the income of the top 1 percent of households
had doubled, family and household incomes have stagnated or
declined for 80 percent of the population."[50] Thus, despite improvements in the economy, these Americans continue to worry
about unemployment and job security, declining real wages, es-
calating medical and housing costs, the availability of affordable
child care programs, the sharp decline in the quality of public education, and crime and drug trafficking in their neighborhoods.

    Furthermore, inequality in the labor market is growing at the
same time that new constraints have emerged on the use of federal resources to address social inequities. The retirement of the
baby boomers over the next twenty to thirty years will increase
the burden on Medicare and Social Security, with powerful consequences for overall tax and spending decisions. Programs ear-
marked for the poor could undergo sharper cuts and even elimination. In addition to new time limits on the receipt of welfare

benefits, public housing and food stamp programs have been cut
for impoverished Americans. Eroding public-sector support for
the poor seems destined to increase pressures for economic survival in the low-wage labor market. Millions of the jobless poor
now receiving welfare assistance are slated to enter the labor
market, where they will compete with the working poor for
available jobs. And, to repeat, even substantial segments of the
middle class have experienced a decline in their living standards.

Also, changes in the American family structure have increased
the need for social and family support among all racial groups.
When I speak of the need for a multiracial coalition to address the
problems of ordinary families, it should be noted that a large segment of such families feature a lone parent. One-quarter of all families and six of every ten black families today are lone-parent families, and most of these lone parents are never-married mothers.[51]
Today, one-half of all marriages end in divorce, and only one-half
of divorced fathers make the payments that they owe by law in support of their children. If current trends continue, one-half of the
children in the United States will experience at least part of their
childhood in a lone-parent family.[52] "Families with multiple earners rise toward the top of the family income distribution, while
families with just one earner fall toward the bottom," observes the
economist James K. Galbraith. "As the number of single-headed
households rises, so too will inequality. This pattern is com-
pounded in the real world by the grim fact that single-headed
households also comprise, to a large extent, those with the most
unstable employment experiences at the lowest hourly wages."[53]

These changes in family structure have been accompanied by
significant changes in work and family responsibilities. Since the

1940s, the proportion of women in the labor force has increased, especially since 1970, when women's rates of labor force participation began to accelerate. In 1950 only one-third of women with a high school education were employed; today two-thirds are working. More than half of women with young children are also working, which is twice as many as two decades ago. And working women tend to do most of their family's housework in spite of their employment outside the home.[54]

In addition to these burdens, women have shouldered increasing responsibility for the care of older relatives. "In the past decade, such caregiving has increased threefold," states pollster Stanley Greenberg; "almost three-quarters of those caring for the elderly are women, two-thirds of whom work outside the home. This is why ordinary Americans are starting to demand a serious debate about social and family support, even as the country's elite are pressing ahead with a long-term bipartisan agenda centered on deficit reduction, entitlement reform, and free trade."[55]

Despite being officially race neutral, programs created in response to these concerns—programs that increase employment opportunities and job skills training, improve public education, promote better child and health care, strengthen supports for working lone-parent families, and reduce neighborhood crime and drug abuse—would profoundly benefit the minority poor, but they would also benefit large segments of the remaining population, including the white majority.

The results of national opinion polls suggest the possibility of a new alignment in support of a comprehensive social rights initiative that would include such programs. If such an alignment is attempted, it should feature a new public rhetoric focused on problems that plague broad segments of the American public—

from the jobless poor to the struggling working and middle classes—and should emphasize integrative programs that would promote the social and economic well-being of all groups. But these groups will have to be effectively mobilized in order to change the current course taken by policy makers. I believe that the best way to accomplish this mobilization is through coalition politics.

Because an effective political coalition in part depends upon how the issues to be addressed are defined, I repeat that it is imperative that the political message underscore the need for economic and social reform that benefits all groups, not just America's minority poor. The framers of this message should be cognizant of the fact that changes in the global economy have increased social inequality and enhanced opportunities for antagonisms between different racial groups. They should also be aware that these groups, although often seen as adversaries, are potential allies in a reform coalition because they suffer from a common problem: economic distress caused by forces beyond their control.

Supporters of a multiracial political coalition would certainly be aided by a broader vision of American race relations. This vision would acknowledge the existence of racial ideology and its past and present impact on the lives of minority individuals and families, but it would also recognize other important social processes that affect the quality of race relations in society and the life chances of individuals and families. I refer not only to the social, economic, and political situations that aggravate racist feelings, but also to a matter that I discuss in the following chapter: namely, the race-neutral global economic forces that affect in varying degrees the lives of all groups, but especially African Americans.

2

GLOBAL ECONOMIC CHANGES AND THE LIMITS OF THE RACE RELATIONS VISION

The Limits of the Race Relations Vision

Despite African Americans' strong focus on the effects of racial discrimination in domestic U.S. employment, their economic fate is inextricably connected with the structure and functioning of a much broader, globally influenced modern economy. Racial bias continues to be an important factor that aggravates black employment problems. Nonetheless, it is important to be aware of the *nonracial* economic forces that have sharply increased joblessness and declining real wages among many African Americans in the last several decades. As the black economist Vivian Henderson argued over two decades ago, racism put blacks in their economic place, but changes in the modern economy have disrupted that place and further restricted opportunities.[1] In this chapter I underline the importance of understanding race-neutral economic forces that create profound effects within all American communities, forces that represent changes in the new economy. I give special attention to the impact of these changes on the African American community to further stimulate thought on coalition building in pursuit of a broad-based economic agenda for ordinary families. Because the economic problems in the black community are often perceived primarily or solely in terms of race—as if they are independent of the race-neutral economic trends affecting families and neighborhoods across the nation—the idea of multiracial coalition building on issues that do not ostensibly involve race is difficult for many to fathom. The remaining sections of this chapter reveal the limits of this vision of race relations.

The Twist in the Demand for Labor

In recent years a "twist" in the demand for different types of labor has occurred. The wedding of emerging technologies and international competition has eroded the basic institutions of the mass production system. In the last several decades, almost all of the improvements in productivity have been associated with technology and human capital, thereby drastically reducing the importance of physical capital and natural resources. The changes in technology that are producing new jobs make many others obsolete.

The workplace has been revolutionized by technological changes that range from the development of robotics to the information highway. Whereas educated workers are at least keeping pace with the increased use of information-based technologies and microcomputers, less sophisticated workers face the growing threat of job displacement in certain industries.[2]

Between 1979 and 1994 the employment-to-population ratio increased by 1 percent for college graduates but declined by 3 percent for high school graduates and by 10 percent for high school dropouts.[3] In the new global economy, highly educated, well-trained men and women are in demand. This may be seen most dramatically in the sharp differences in employment experiences among American males. Unlike men with lower levels of education, college-educated men are working more, not less.[4]

The shift in the demand for labor has been especially devastating for those low-skilled workers whose incorporation into the mainstream economy has been marginal or recent. Even before the economic restructuring of the nation's economy, low-skilled African Americans were at the end of the employment line, often the last to be hired and the first to be let go. The economic situation for many blacks has now been further weakened because they tend not only to reside in communities that have higher jobless rates and lower employment growth, but also to lack access to areas of higher employment and job growth.[5]

Of all the changes in the economy that have adversely affected low-skilled African American workers, perhaps the most significant have been those in the manufacturing sector. One study revealed that in the 1970s "up to half of the huge employment declines for less-educated blacks might be explained by industrial shifts away from manufacturing toward other sectors."[6] The manufacturing losses in some northern cities have been staggering. In the twenty-year period from 1967 to 1987, Philadelphia lost 64 percent of its manufacturing jobs; Chicago lost 60 percent;

New York City, 58 percent; and Detroit, 51 percent. In absolute numbers, these percentages represent the loss of 160,000 jobs in Philadelphia, 326,000 in Chicago, 520,000—over half a million— in New York, and 108,000 in Detroit.[7]

Another study examined the effects of economic restructuring in the 1980s by highlighting the changes in blue-collar employment's variety and quality (measured in terms of earnings, benefits, union protection, and involuntary part-time employment). The authors found that both relative earnings and employment rates among unskilled black workers were lower than in previous years. Two reasons were given: a decline in the number of jobs that traditionally provided a living wage (the high-wage blue-collar cluster, roughly 50 percent of which were manufacturing jobs) and a decline in the quality of secondary jobs on which these workers increasingly had to rely. The result was lower relative earnings for the remaining workers in the labor market. As employment prospects worsened throughout the 1980s, rising proportions of low-skilled black workers dropped out of the legitimate labor market.[8]

Although blue-collar workers from all groups have suffered, industrial restructuring has had especially severe consequences for African American communities across the nation. "As late as the 1968–70 period," states John Kasarda, "more than 70 percent of all blacks working in metropolitan areas held blue-collar jobs at the same time that more than 50 percent of all metropolitan workers held white-collar jobs. Moreover, of the large numbers of urban blacks classified as blue-collar workers during the late 1960s, more than half were employed in goods-producing industries."[9]

The number of employed black males ages twenty to twenty-nine working in manufacturing industries fell dramatically between 1973 and 1987 (from three of every eight to one in five). Meanwhile, the share of employed young black men in the retail trade and service jobs rose sharply (from 17 to almost 27 percent and from 10 to nearly 21 percent, respectively). This shift in opportunities was not without economic consequences: in 1987 the average annual earnings of twenty- to twenty-nine-year-old males who held jobs in the retail trade and service sectors were 25 to 30 percent less than those of males employed in manufacturing sectors.[10]

The structural shift in the distribution of industrial job opportunities is not the only reason for declining earnings among young black male workers. Important changes in the patterns of occupational staffing within firms and industries, including those in manufacturing, are also to blame. Substantial numbers of new professional, technical, and managerial positions have been created that primarily benefit those with higher levels of formal education. Because such jobs require at least some education beyond high school, young dropouts and even high school graduates "have faced a dwindling supply of career jobs offering the real earnings opportunities available to them in the 1960s and early 1970s."[11]

Most of the new jobs for workers with limited training and education are in the service sector and are disproportionately held by women. This is even truer for those who work in social services, which include the industries of health, education, and welfare. Within central cities the number of jobs for less-educated workers has declined precipitously. However, many

workers stayed afloat thanks to jobs in the expanding social service sector, especially black women who had some years of high
school but no diploma. Among all women workers, the proportion employed in social services climbed between 1979 and 1993
(from 28 to 33 percent). The health and education industries ab-
sorbed nearly all of this increase. Of the 54 million female workers in 1993, almost one-third were employed in social service industries. On balance, social services tend to feature a more
highly educated workforce. Only 20 percent of all female workers with less than a high school degree were employed in social
services in 1993. (The figure for males of comparable education
is even less. Only 4 percent of employed less-educated men held
social service jobs in 1993, although within central cities the figure for black men rose to 12 percent.) Nonetheless, the proportion of less-educated female workers in social services was notably higher than in 1989.[12]

Indeed, despite the relatively higher educational level of social
service workers, 37 percent of employed less-educated black
women in central cities worked in social services in 1993, holding jobs largely in hospitals, elementary schools, nursing care,
and child care. In central cities in the largest metropolitan areas,
the fraction of African American female workers with low levels
of education sharply increased in social services, from 30.5 percent in 1979 to 40.5 percent in 1993.[13] Clearly, less-educated
black female workers have depended heavily on social service
employment. Given the overall decline of jobs for less-educated
central-city workers, the opportunity for employment in the social service industries kept many inner-city workers from the
growing ranks of the jobless.

The Computer Revolution
and the Changing Demand for Labor

The computer revolution is a major reason for the shift in the demand for skilled workers. Whereas only one-quarter of American workers directly used a computer in their jobs in 1983, by 1993 that figure had risen to almost half the workforce. According to the economist Alan Krueger, "The expansion of computer use can account for one-third to two-thirds of the increase in the payoff to education between 1984 and 1993 [in the United States]."[14] Two reasons for this increased payoff are cited: first, even after a number of background factors, such as experience and education, are taken into account, those who use computers at work tend to be paid more than those who do not; second, the industries with the greatest shift in employment toward more highly skilled workers are those in which computer technology is more intensively used. As shown in figure 7, the share of workers with college degrees increased most sharply in the industries with the most rapid expansion of computer use.

Early studies of the diffusion of computer technology have revealed a strong positive relationship between computer ownership and income and education. And although systematic research is lacking, it is clear that in jobless ghetto areas and depressed rural areas computerization and telecommunications are severely underdeveloped.

A recent study illustrates how lack of access to key technological resources can be predicted along race and class lines, specifically in relation to ownership of home computers. In this study 73 percent of white students lived in households with a home computer, whereas only 32 percent of black students did so.

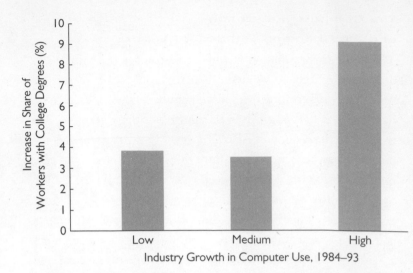

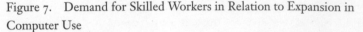

Figure 7.   Demand for Skilled Workers in Relation to Expansion in Computer Use

Source: Adapted from Alan B. Krueger, "What's Up with Wages?" Mimeo from the Industrial Relations Section, Princeton University, 1997.

Overall, 44.2 percent of the white respondents owned a computer at home, compared with 29 percent of black respondents. The authors found, however, that household income rather than race explained home computer ownership—levels of income correspond to the probability of owning a computer at home, regardless of race.[15]

Nonetheless, because the proportion of higher-income blacks to all blacks is considerably lower than the proportion of higher-income whites to all whites, the problem of computer access for blacks as a group is more serious. Further, because the cited study was based on a nationwide telephone survey instead of in-person door-to-door interviews, it quite probably underestimates the lack of computer access among the most disadvantaged Americans. Because many of the poorest Americans do not own telephones, they are beyond the scope of such investigations.

Rising opportunities for computer-literate workers have helped compensate for declining demands for workers in other sectors of the economy. And it appears that the overwhelming majority of all new jobs will require at least some computer skills.[16] This means that, without access to computers, many of the nation's have-nots—and especially the minority have-nots—are in danger of becoming permanent economic proletarians.

The Effects of the Global Economy

The shift in demand for skilled versus low-skilled workers can also be related to the growing internationalization of economic activity, including increased trade with countries that have large numbers of low-skilled, low-wage workers.[17] Two developments facilitated the growth in global economic activity: (1) advances in information and communications technologies, which significantly lowered transportation and communication costs and thereby encouraged companies to shift work to low-wage areas around the world; and (2) the expansion of free trade, which reduced the price of imports and raised the output of export industries.[18]

The increased output of export industries aids skilled workers, simply because skilled workers are heavily represented in export industries. But increasing imports that compete with labor-intensive industries (for example, apparel, textile, toys, footwear, and some manufacturing) hurt unskilled labor.[19] "As a share of the U.S. economy, trade has been expanding since the late 1960s," asserts the economist James K. Galbraith, "and imports of manufacturing from developing countries, in particular, grew dramatically in the early 1980s."[20] According to economic theory, the expansion of trade with countries that have a large proportion of relatively unskilled labor will result in downward pressure on the wages of low-skilled American workers because it will lower the prices of the goods they produce.

Alan Krueger reflects:

Whatever the role that trade has played in the past, I suspect that trade will place greater pressure on low-skilled workers in the future. The reason for this suspicion is simply that there are a great many unskilled workers in the world who are paid very little. One and a half billion potential workers have left schools before they reached age 13; half the world's workers leave at age 16 or earlier. When these workers are brought into global economic competition (because of greater openness, more political stability, and greater investment in developing countries), the consequences are unlikely to be positive for low-skilled workers in developed countries.[21]

Because of the concentration of low-skilled black workers in vulnerable labor-intensive industries (for example, 40 percent of the workforce in the apparel industry is African American), developments in international trade are likely to adversely affect their employment prospects.[22]

The Effects of Supply-Side Factors

The factors contributing to the relative decline in the economic status of low-skilled workers are not found only on the demand side. In the 1980s the growing wage differential was also related to two supply-side factors—the decline in the relative supply of college graduates and the influx of poor immigrants. "In the 1970s the relative supply of college graduates grew rapidly, the result of the baby boomers who enrolled in college in the late 1960s and early 1970s in response to the high rewards for college degrees and fear of being drafted for the Vietnam war," state Freeman and Katz. "The growth in supply overwhelmed the increase in demand for more educated workers, and the returns to college diminished."[23] In the 1980s, the returns to college increased because college enrollment rates stopped rising, thereby contributing to the decade's rapid growth in income and wage inequality. (However, in the 1990s college enrollment rates have risen again.)

Also in the 1980s, a large number of immigrants with little formal education from developing countries arrived in the United States and affected the wages of low-educated native workers, particularly the high school dropouts. According to one estimate, one-third of the decline in earnings for male high school dropouts compared with other workers in the 1980s may be due to immigration.[24] Of course, increased immigration is only one of several factors contributing to growing inequality. As Sheldon Danziger and Peter Gottschalk appropriately point out, "Immigrants are heavily concentrated in a few states, such as California and Florida. . . . [I]nequality did rise in these states, but it rose in most areas, even those with few immigrants."[25]

Low-Skilled Workers and Slow Wage Growth

The decreased relative demand for low-skilled workers has contributed to the growing wage inequality discussed in chapter 1. But
the general slowdown in average real wage growth has also contributed to their economic woes. Although low-skilled workers
have experienced the greatest declines in their inflation-adjusted
earnings, most Americans in the workforce have seen an erosion of
their real annual household income because of declining real wage
growth. Even though the economy grew by almost 3 percent between 1995 and 1998, since 1973 it has averaged only 2.2 percent
in annual growth. Such seemingly tiny increases matter a great
deal. If we had experienced a half percent annual higher economic
growth since 1973, we would have generated nearly 300 billion additional dollars in federal tax revenue without an increase in tax
rates. That added revenue would have precluded the debate over
deficit reduction and service cutbacks that dominated American
political life throughout the 1980s and first half of the 1990s.[26]

The slowdown in economic growth that began in the 1970s is
undoubtedly tied to the slowdown in productivity growth. "Economists of all stripes agree that the nation's standard of living is not
determined by job growth, low unemployment, low inflation, or
the surging Dow Jones, as important as those factors are," states
Henry R. Richmond, "but by annual productivity growth. This is
because productivity growth is the key to per capita income growth
and economic growth generally that does not trigger inflation."[27]

As Alan Krueger puts it, "A country can only pay out in wages
and profits what it produces."[28] Although the distribution of
wages and profits varies over time, productivity growth determines the size of the economic pie to be distributed. However, in
the last twenty-five years, productivity growth has slowed, low-

ering America's standard of living. Productivity growth averaged only 1.1 percent from 1973 to 1995, less than half the annual growth of 2.3 percent since the Civil War, and significantly below the 1.9 percent annual average since 1909. Between 1989 and 1995 annual productivity was even lower—0.9 percent. The result is a smaller economic pie and lower household incomes.[29]

Economists are mystified about the causes of the slowdown in productivity growth that began in the early 1970s and lasted until the late 1990s.* What is clear, however, is that the slowdown

---

*In the first quarter of 1999 growth in nonfarm productivity surged at a 4 percent annual rate, providing evidence that productivity is perking up after a 25-year slumber. Some observers have wondered about the relationship between productivity growth and the increased use of computers. Alan Krueger has commented thoughtfully on this issue:

> The effect of computers on worker productivity remains a controversial issue. Several early studies found at most a weak association between computers and productivity (e.g., Baily and Gordon, 1988). Significantly, the unprecedented growth of computer power in the last two decades coincided with a slowdown in productivity growth. Why would companies invest so much money in computer technology if it hasn't raised productivity? What could cause this paradox? Several recent studies have found a positive effect of computers on productivity at the firm and industry level, so there may be less of a paradox here than previously believed. But if computers have led to greater output per worker, why wasn't aggregate productivity growth greater in the 1980s? In a recent paper, Oliner and Sichel (1994) argue persuasively that the spread of computers and related technology represent just 2 percent of the capital stock. For example, if computers raise the productivity of workers who use them 15%, then the 25 percentage point increase in the proportion of workers using computers between 1984 and 1993 would increase productivity by just

in wage growth during this period stems from the slowdown in productivity growth. But to account fully for the "recent period of unusually slow real wage growth" several factors in addition to productivity growth must be considered. One is the blossoming of the temporary work industry. Although the temporary work industry accounts for only slightly more than 10 percent of the rise in employment during the economic recovery period of the 1990s, the growth of this industry "could help companies to fill bottlenecks when they arise, without resorting to raising the entire wage schedule."[30] Another factor may be the delinking of wages. Wages across groups of workers in a given industry are not as linked as in previous years. There have been fewer across-the-board wage increases during the 1990 period of economic recovery than in previous periods of recovery. Further factors include the specter of downsizing, which may have led employees to moderate their demands for higher wages, and the technological change and trade that have reduced labor's share and increased capital's share of national output. Moreover, the decrease in the real value of the minimum wage has had a particular effect on the wage growth of unskilled workers, and the dramatic and persistent decline of union membership in the private sector (from more than 35 percent in the 1960s to only 10 percent in 1996) has weakened workers' bargaining power for wage increases.[31]*

0.4% per year [Alan Krueger, "Consequences of Computerization of the Workplace" (paper for "Research, Technology and Employment" conference, organized by the Spanish Presidency of the Council of the European Union, December 6–8, 1995), 5].

*Arguments concerning changes in labor and capital's share of national output are controversial because of difficulties in measuring

These changes have affected the wages of workers across racial lines. However, the relative wage declines have been greatest among the less-educated and the untrained workers. Accordingly, the racial or ethnic groups with the highest proportion of low-skilled workers, such as African Americans, are disproportionately represented in the distribution of American workers suffering the greatest economic stresses. This troubling problem is clearly evident among many black central-city residents.

Shifts in Labor Demand and
Black Central-City Residents

As urban economies have been transformed from goods production to information processing, black central-city residents with no education beyond high school have been increasingly displaced from mainstream employment. For example, the unemployment rates for central-city black males with only a high school diploma climbed in midwestern cities from 11 percent in the late 1960s to 41 percent in the early 1990s, in northeastern

----

labor's share. According to the conventional measure, there was no change in labor's share of national output in the 1980s. But the conventional measure relies on data that includes Bill Gates as a worker. A recent paper by Alan Krueger includes a method of decomposing labor compensation into a component due to human capital and a component due to "raw labor." With this alternative measure, Krueger finds that only 5 percent of national income is due to raw labor, down from about 15 percent in the 1960s. (See Alan B. Krueger, "Measuring Labor's Share," Working Paper no. 413, Industrial Relations Section, Princeton University, January 1999.)

cities from 10 percent to 31 percent, and in southern cities from 10 to 22 percent.[32]

With the transition from manufacturing to services, cognitive and interpersonal skills have become prerequisites even for many low-paying jobs. Surveying 3,000 employers in Atlanta, Boston, and Los Angeles, the economist Harry Holzer of Michigan State University found that only 5 to 10 percent of the jobs in central-city areas for workers who are *not* college graduates require few work credentials or cognitive skills. This means that not only do most inner-city workers today need to have the basic skills of reading, writing, and arithmetic, but they need to know how to operate a computer as well. Also, most employers require a high school degree, particular kinds of previous work experience, and job references. Because of the large oversupply of low-skilled workers relative to the number of low-skilled jobs, many low-educated and poorly trained individuals have difficulty finding jobs even when the local labor market is strong.[33]

The problem is that in recent years tight labor markets have been of relatively short duration, frequently followed by recessions that either wiped out previous gains for many workers or did not allow others to fully recover from a previous period of economic stagnation. It would take sustained tight labor markets over many years to draw back those discouraged inner-city workers who have dropped out of the labor market altogether, some for very long periods of time.

However, at the time of this writing, the nation is in one of the longest economic recoveries in the last half century, a recovery that has lasted nine years and generated 18 million net new jobs and the lowest official unemployment rate in thirty years. This sustained recovery is beginning to have positive effects on

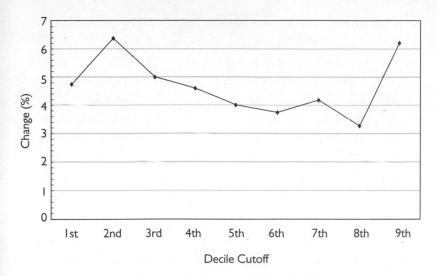

Figure 8.   Change in Real Hourly Wages for Male Workers,
1996–1998
Source: Economic Policy Institute.

low-skilled workers, including the hard-core unemployed. The
ranks of those out of work for more than six months declined by
almost 150,000 over a two-month period in early 1997. And the
unemployment rate for high school dropouts declined by five
points, from 12 to 7 percent, from 1992 to early 1998. Two-fifths
of this decline occurred since 1997.[34] Finally, as shown in figure
8, real wage growth was quite impressive in 1997 and 1998, especially for low-wage workers. Except for male workers at the
ninth decile cutoff (ninetieth percentile) of the wage distribution,
those at the bottom three decile cutoffs (thirtieth percentile and
below) experienced the highest percentage hourly wage increase
from 1996 to 1998 (ranging from 4.7 to 6.4 percent). Increases in

the minimum wage and the unexpectedly low inflation help to account for some of this wage growth, but the prolonged strong economy undoubtedly contributed.

How long this current period of economic recovery will last is anybody's guess. Some economists feel that it will last for at least several more years. If it does, it will be the best antidote for low-skilled workers whose employment and earning prospects have been diminished in the late twentieth century. For example, in America's inner cities the extension of the economic recovery for several more years will significantly lower the overall jobless rate not only for low-skilled workers still in the labor force but also for those who have been outside the labor market for many years. In addition, it will enhance the job prospects of many welfare recipients who reach the time limit on welfare receipt.

But given the decrease in relative demand for low-skilled labor, what will happen to all of these groups if the economy slows down and we are faced with a new recession or a period of economic stagnation? Considering the changing nature of the economy, unless a concerted effort is made to increase their skills, there is little reason to assume that their long-term prospects will be anything but bleak. Why? Because the economic trend that has twisted against low-skilled workers is unlikely to reverse itself. Despite the muting of this trend during the prolonged recovery, in the long term their job prospects and earnings are diminished.

However, increasing the skills of inner-city workers is only part of the challenge. Many central-city job applicants are physically isolated from places of employment and socially isolated from the informal job networks that have become a major source of job placement. The growing suburbanization of jobs, both in manufacturing and services, has isolated inner-city minorities from many work opportunities. Labor markets today, unlike previous years, are mainly regional, and long commutes in automobiles are common. Most ghetto residents do not have access to an automobile and therefore have to rely on public transit systems that make the connection between inner-city neighborhoods and suburban job locations difficult and time-consuming. To make matters worse, many inner-city residents lack information or knowledge about suburban job opportunities. In the segregated inner-city ghettos, the breakdown of the informal job information network aggravates the problems of spatial job mismatch.[35]

Toward a More Holistic View of the African American Economic Experience

In the foregoing analysis I have tried to relate many of the economic woes in the African American community to fundamental shifts in the demand for labor in the global economy. Whereas the more educated and highly trained African Americans, like their counterparts among other racial groups, have very likely benefited from the shifts in labor demand, those with lesser skills have suffered.

It is important to note that in the United States the sharp decline in the relative demand for low-skilled labor has had a more adverse effect on blacks than on whites because a substantially larger proportion of African Americans is unskilled. Although the number of skilled blacks (including managers, professionals, and technicians) has increased sharply in the last several years, the proportion of those who are unskilled remains large. This is because the black population, burdened by cumulative experiences of racial restrictions, was overwhelmingly unskilled just several decades ago.[36]*

Although racial discrimination and segregation exacerbate the labor market problems of low-skilled African Americans, we must not lose sight of the fact that many of these problems are currently driven by fundamental changes in the new global economy. Nonetheless, there is a tendency among policy makers, scholars, and black leaders to view economic problems in the black community separately from the national and international trends affecting American families and neighborhoods. If the economic problems of the African American community are defined solely in racial terms, they can be isolated and viewed as requiring only race-based solutions, such as those proposed by the

*One way to measure the adverse effects of the decreased relative demand for low-skilled labor on blacks is to determine the relationship between the return to skills and the size of the racial wage gap. Recent research indicates that the well-documented convergence of the black and white wage rates between 1940 and 1980 slowed in the 1980s. The research reveals that a substantial part of this slowdown in convergence is due to the rising demand for skilled labor in combination with the disproportionate concentration of blacks in the lower half of the skill distribution. (See Chinhui Juhn, Kevin M. Murphy, and Brooks Pierce, "Accounting for the Slowdown in Black-White Convergence," in *Workers and Their Wages: Changing Patterns in the United States,* edited by Marvin H. Kosters [Washington, D.C.: American Enterprise Institute Press, 1991]; also David Card and Thomas Lemieux, "Changing Wage Structure and Black-White Wage Differentials among Men and Women: A Longitudinal Analysis," *Working Paper Series,* Working Paper no. 4755 [Cambridge, Mass.: National Bureau of Economic Research, May 1994].)

Left, or narrow political solutions with subtle racial connotations, such as welfare reform, as proposed by the Right. If leaders in the African American community perceive the economic problems of black people as separate from the national and international trends affecting ordinary American families, they will be less likely to see the need to join forces with other groups seeking economic reform.*

Vivian Henderson warned the nation against this short-sighted vision in 1975. "The economic future of blacks in the United States is bound up with that of the rest of the nation," he argued. "Politics designed in the future to cope with the problems of the poor and victimized will also yield benefits to blacks. In contrast, any efforts to treat blacks separately from the rest of the nation are likely to lead to frustration, heightened racial animosities, and a

---

*It is important to note that many African American leaders, including Bayard Rustin, A. Philip Randolph, Martin Luther King Jr., Whitney M. Young Jr., and Jesse Jackson recognized the need to move beyond race-specific issues and join forces with other groups seeking economic reform. Jesse Jackson's National Rainbow Coalition, created in the 1980s when he sought the Democratic presidential nomination in 1984 and 1988, is the latest notable example. The National Rainbow Coalition attempted to resolve many of the objectives I have outlined for a national multiracial coalition. However, the National Rainbow Coalition never really captured the imagination of broad segments of the population. Jackson's messages bounced from race-neutral themes that resonated with all groups to race-specific themes (such as minority set asides) that drew the attention of minority populations.

For a good historical discussion of the involvement of black leaders in "larger" socioeconomic issues, see Dona Cooper Hamilton and Charles V. Hamilton, *Race and Social Welfare Policies of Civil Rights Organizations* (New York: Columbia University Press, 1997).

waste of the country's resources and the precious resources of black people."[37]

If alive today, he would probably agree strongly with the argument that no group in the United States would benefit more than African Americans from the creation of a progressive multiracial political coalition. Without such a coalition, there will be little chance of developing and effectively pursuing a mass-based economic agenda to mute the effects of global economic change on ordinary families.

3

BUILDING A FOUNDATION FOR MULTIRACIAL COOPERATION

The Constituency for a Multiracial Political Coalition

As the new global economy creates growing inequality in the labor market and increasing economic and emotional stresses for ordinary families, including those where the working mother is the only parent, many of the policies and actions of the government do more to aggravate than alleviate their economic woes. I have in mind trade policies that facilitate the pursuit of cheap labor in the global marketplace, monetary policies that elevate real interest rates and thereby lower employment rates, tax policies that favor the truly wealthy, and partisan opposition to programs of public investment and national health insurance.

The University of Texas economist James K. Galbraith reminds us of the more enviable position of workers vis-à-vis the government that existed several decades ago:

From 1945 through 1970, the state maintained a wide range
of protections for low-wage, less educated, more vulnerable
workers, so that a broadly equal pattern of social progress
was sustained despite, even in those distant years, rapid technological change. These protections were held in place by a
stable macroeconomic policy that avoided sharp or prolonged disruptions to economic growth, and in particular by
a monetary policy that was subordinated to these larger objectives. In those years, the government *as a whole* was committed to the pursuit of full employment, price stability, and
high rates of economic growth. Following 1970, technological change continued, but the protections were withdrawn,
and at the same time macroeconomic policy became much
more unstable. The state shifted its support from the economy in general, the macroeconomy, to specific leading sectors of the economy—in fact, to the firms and industries
most devoted to technological change. Monetary policy led
the way, by declaring its independence from the larger objectives of economic policy, and its responsibility for the defeat
of inflation above all other economic goals.[1]

Moreover, the "Reagan experiment" operated under the assumption that in order to increase productivity and economic
growth and reduce prices, unemployment, and poverty, the government should avoid active interventions in domestic policies.
This experiment resulted in historic and profound changes in tax
and transfer policies in the 1980s. The rapid inflation of the
1970s had already eroded the real value of many transfer benefits
and pushed lower- and middle-income wage earners into higher
marginal tax brackets. To make matters worse, the tax structure
became even more regressive, featuring an increase in Social Se-

curity taxes, on top of regressive taxes on wages, and a diminished progressivity of the taxes on total income.[2]

"Given the large increase in market inequality in the 1980s," state the economists Sheldon Danziger and Peter Gottschalk, "government tax and transfer policies would have had to become more redistributed than they were in the 1970s just to keep post-tax, post-transfer inequality constant. Instead, tax and transfer policy changes became less effective in reducing market inequality. As a result, post-tax and transfer inequality increased by even more than market inequality."[3] Although the Tax Reform Act of 1986 and the Omnibus Budget Reconciliation Act of 1990 represent attempts to redistribute income progressively, the changes "were barely noticeable."[4]

There have been other recent government efforts to ease the burdens on vulnerable families, such as the expansions of the earned income tax credit (EITC) in 1986, 1990, and 1993, and the Family and Medical Leave Act of 1993 (FMLA). The EITC is a wage subsidy for the working poor, and its expansions reflected a recognition, even under the Bush and Reagan administrations, of the erosion of wages for low-paid work and the weakening of other policies to help the working poor, such as the minimum wage. The FMLA was designed to partially alleviate the conflicts involving family and work experienced by a growing number of Americans. Under the FMLA, workers are allowed to take up to twelve weeks of unpaid leave for the birth or adoption of a child and for illness, including the illness of a spouse or parent. However, even these modest proposals have been hotly debated in Congress. The traditional bipartisan support for the EITC has begun to erode in the Republican-controlled Congress, so much so that the Senate passed a budget resolution in

1995 that assumed cuts in the EITC by roughly 21 billion dollars over seven years. And the FMLA was initially vetoed by President Bush.*

A multiracial political coalition could generate an earnest national debate on Congress's current approach to domestic policies and prompt public officials to consider seriously the effects of their action or inaction on a broad range of issues that impact vulnerable families. Take, for example, the issue of trade liberalization policies. Although the overall impact of trade liberalization legislation continues to be debated by economists, it appears

---

*Francine D. Blau, Marianne A. Ferber, and Anne E. Winkler point out in this connection that opponents of the FMLA "tended to ignore or minimize the potential benefits of leaves for employers and were particularly concerned about the cost imposed on them, since they continue to pay for health insurance for workers on leave and must bear the costs of training replacement workers. Pay for replacement workers, however, is not an added cost because workers on leave do not draw a paycheck. Moreover, there are benefits. . . . Family leave lowers the cost of turnover, which can be quite substantial when training and moving expenses are considered. Also, it may enhance workers' commitment to the firm and hence their productivity. In fact, a recent study found that providing such unpaid leaves to employees is less expensive for employers than replacing workers who are forced to resign because such leaves are not available. This suggests that the cost of providing short, unpaid family leave is not likely to be unduly onerous for business. International evidence also indicates that, at least thus far, parental leave has not caused the severe problems for firms that had been anticipated by some critics" (Francine D. Blau, Marianne A. Ferber, and Anne E. Winkler, *The Economics of Women, Men, and Work*, 3d ed. [Upper Saddle River, N.J.: Prentice Hall, 1998], 315).

to me to be an ideal issue around which to organize a national dialogue on policies that may adversely affect ordinary families.

It is true that liberalized trade has increased exports in areas
such as the aerospace industry, with beneficial effects for highly
skilled workers. At the same time, increasing imports that compete with labor-intensive industries (such as apparel, textile, toys,
footwear, and some manufacturing industries) hurt low-skilled
labor.[5] This is one of the issues raised by House Democrats who
in 1997 and again in 1998 voted overwhelmingly against President Clinton's "fast-track" proposal on free trade. The legislation that the president introduced was written to attract Republican support. It therefore did not include the labor and
environmental protection standards demanded by Democrats
and their allies—union leaders and environmentalists.[6]

The Democrats were not persuaded by Clinton's argument
that Americans stand to gain from an economy dominated by
high technology and an educated workforce. The House Democrats argued instead that blue-collar workers would be forced
into a "race to the bottom" through competition with developing countries that lack the labor laws and environmental protections that have evolved in the United States. As House Minority
leader Richard Gephardt put it, the question is not *whether* to
trade, since we all know that trade is important for the overall
health and growth of the economy. The question is *how* to trade.
Moreover, union leaders, often branded as protectionist, indicated that they would not have opposed the fast-track legislation
if it had guaranteed workplace and environmental rights. As
Frank Borgers, a professor of labor relations at the University of
Massachusetts, put it: "If you raise labor standards in low-wage

countries, that's good for them and good for us. It would slow the exodus of jobs."[7]

During debates on the fast-track trade bill in 1997, the vast majority of Democrats in the House of Representatives told Clinton that "American trade policy is skewed in the wrong direction. They sought to equalize the terms of competition between workers in the United States and other countries rather than focus on protecting intellectual property rights or other corporate interests."[8]

An intergroup coalition of organized labor, environmental groups, and Hispanic organizations, including the Hispanic caucus in the House of Representatives, fought against the president's bill on free trade. Black leaders such as Maxine Waters, John Lewis, and Jesse Jackson were involved in this debate, but their efforts were not highly visible. If the proposed fast-track legislation of trade would increase the displacement of low-skilled labor in this country, it would create enormous problems for the large proportion of unskilled African American workers.

Issues that are defined explicitly in racial terms understandably attract more attention from black leaders. But it is important that black leaders expand their vision and address race-neutral issues that significantly affect the African American community with the same degree of attention they give to race-specific issues.

The displacement problems associated with free trade are a race-neutral issue that ought to bring together the swelling ranks of have-not Americans—that is, the low- to moderate-income groups of any race—in an important and constructive dialogue on national economic policy. At the time of this writing, the fast-track trade bill has once again been defeated in the House of Representatives, but the pressure to open U.S. markets to goods produced cheaply in countries that lack reasonable safety, wage, and environmental standards for their workers is unlikely to abate.

As we think about other issues of national economic policy that affect low- to moderate-income families and that ought to engage different racial groups in a national dialogue, one issue immediately comes to mind: the need to generate national support for achieving and maintaining tight labor markets—in other words, full employment.

Such a goal by definition challenges the monetary policies supported by Wall Street, policies by which the Federal Reserve Board, concerned with keeping inflation in check, keeps labor markets from tightening by maintaining or creating high interest rates: as interests rates rise, unemployment rates climb.

In a critical assessment of this approach, Galbraith points out that the principal causes of the rising inequality in the wage structure

> lie in the hard blows of recession, unemployment, and slow economic growth, combined with the effects of inflation and political resistance to rising real value of the minimum wage. These are blows that, when once delivered, are not erased in any short period of economic recovery. They can be reversed, and in American history have been reversed, only by sustained periods of full employment alongside controlled inflation and a determined drive toward social justice. We last saw such a movement in this country in the 1960s, and before that only during World War II.[9]

However, Galbraith goes on to point out that beginning in 1970 the government's goal of full employment was abandoned in favor of fighting inflation. The only instrument deemed suitable for this purpose was high interest rates produced by the Federal Reserve. Unfortunately for the average worker, high interest rates elevate unemployment.[10]

As the economic analyst Jeff Faux has pointed out, this is a value issue. The Federal Reserve Board "protects the value of financial assets over the value of jobs by consistently overestimating the level of unemployment necessary to retain price stability."[11] Economists are not sure what constitutes the right level of unemployment to stabilize prices. But in the last few years, when tighter labor markets have failed to trigger inflation, the opinions of the financial pundits have consistently been wrong on this question.[12]

A powerful multiracial coalition that included the swelling ranks of the low- to moderate-income have-nots could, as a part of its national agenda, demand that the president appoint, and Congress approve, members to the Federal Reserve Board who will ensure that it upholds "its mandate to pursue both high employment and price stability by probing much more forcefully the limits of the economy's capacity to produce without inflation."[13] Policies that are effective in promoting full employment and controlling inflation would likely draw the support of the more advantaged, higher-income members of society as well. Currently, the discussion of how to control inflation is a complex one that involves mainly intellectual and financial elites. But I think that Jeff Faux is absolutely correct when he argues that "Americans are more likely to participate in a national debate over what it takes to achieve full employment than in the current dispiriting argument over how many people must be denied work in order to make the bond market comfortable."[14]

Such a debate over employment policies would be greatly facilitated if we were able to overcome our racial divisions and develop and coordinate local grassroots organizations that could join established national leaders—or generate new ones—in a powerful political coalition. This coalition could pursue policy issues relevant to all members of the large have-not population. But issues pursued by such a coalition do not have to be limited to those that address the problems of lower- to moderate-income groups. A standing coalition would also be poised to join forces with other groups to address particular issues that affect broader segments of population across race and class lines.

Let me give a quick example. It is generally recognized that public investment in core infrastructure improvements in roads, transit, sewers, and utilities is important for private investment. Indeed, private investment relies heavily on core infrastructure maintenance and improvement.[15] What is not generally recognized is that core infrastructure investments, in turn, are dependent on factors of density and distance for their initial feasibility and efficient operation. However, urban sprawl has made public investment in core infrastructure more costly and difficult. From 1970 to 1990, the urbanized area of American metropolitan regions expanded from eight to fifteen times as fast as population growth. From 1973 to 1996, as sprawl intensified, the growth in the value of core infrastructure plummeted.[16]

The strains that urban sprawl places on the core infrastructure are felt in many ways. As industrial and residential development sprawls across an ever-broadening geographical area, it creates a situation in which the urban economy is inadequately supported, as more transportation costs and inefficiency are imposed on business, more urban minorities are further removed from access to jobs, and more pollution and destruction of natural resources occur over a wider area.[17]

In Portland, Oregon, public discussion of the adverse effects of urban sprawl on the quality of metropolitan life led to the passage of zoning laws to control urban sprawl. It seems to me that an ongoing public discussion of the effects of urban sprawl on families, institutions, and neighborhoods could bring together groups not only from different racial backgrounds, but from different economic class backgrounds as well.

Generating Interracial Cooperation and Coalition Building

Given the complex national and international economic changes that affect broad segments of the American population, the development of a progressive multiracial political coalition is more important now than ever. As long as groups affected by global economic changes reject or fail to consider or envision the need for mutual political cooperation, they stand little chance of generating the political muscle needed to ease their economic burdens. The case for a progressive multiracial political coalition has to be made in political messages that resonate with broad segments of the American population. And the effectiveness of these messages will depend in part upon how we define the issues to be addressed.

The political message calling for change and outlining the need for a multiracial coalition ought to emphasize the benefits that would accrue to all groups who are struggling economically in America, not just poor minorities. The message should encompass the idea that changes in the global economy have enhanced social inequality and created situations that have heightened antagonisms between different racial and ethnic groups, and that although these groups are seen as social adversaries, they are potential allies in a reform coalition. Why? Because they are all negatively affected more or less by impersonal global economic changes.

Given the racial friction that has marred intergroup interaction in urban America, the formation of a multiracial reform coalition presents a challenge. Indeed, the contemporary emphasis on racial division and racial ideology makes it difficult to promote the idea of a multiracial political coalition to develop and pursue a mass-based economic agenda. Beginning with the riots in Los Angeles in 1992, and especially after the 1995 O.J. Simpson murder trial, media attention to racial matters has highlighted those factors that divide us.

Although it is important to acknowledge the racial divisions in America so that they can be meaningfully addressed, the incessant attention given to these gaps has obscured the following fact: black, white, Latino, Asian, and Native Americans share many concerns, are besieged by many similar problems, and have important norms, values, and aspirations in common. Take the issue of values. An analysis of the responses to questions that were variously asked in the national surveys conducted by National Opinion Research Center's General Social Survey since 1982 reveals only marginal racial differences in core values pertaining to work, education, family, religion, law enforcement, and civic duty. For example, in a 1982 survey 90 percent of whites and 89 percent of blacks felt that one's own family and children are very important; in a 1984 survey 88 percent of whites and 95 percent of blacks felt that the obligation of American citizens to do community service is very or somewhat important; and in a 1993 survey 95 percent of whites and 92 percent of blacks felt that hard work in achieving life outcomes is either important or very important, and 97 percent of blacks and 88 percent of whites supported the view that being self-sufficient was either very important or one of the most important things in life.*

Also consider the perception of problems. As revealed in table 1, questions about whether problems pertaining to public schools, jobs, affordable housing, families, and health care were getting worse or harder for the people with whom the respondents identify ("people like you or families like yours") elicited considerable agreement across racial and ethnic groups.

Furthermore, consider views on major policy issues. As seen in table 2, except for affirmative action and abortion, there are no notable differences across racial and ethnic groups on reported

*Findings from the General Surveys of the National Opinion Research Center of the University of Chicago. Considering the prevailing stereotypes, the findings on self-sufficiency are counterintuitive. Although there is a 9 percent racial gap, an overwhelming majority of respondents from both races strongly supported the idea of self-sufficiency. The only other finding that should be mentioned pertains to views on the importance of being married. Whereas 43 percent of the black respondents felt that being married was very important or one of the most important things in life, 53 percent of the white respondents felt this way.

TABLE 1   ARE THE PROBLEMS OF PEOPLE LIKE YOU
(OR FAMILIES LIKE YOURS) GETTING WORSE?

	Percent Saying "Worse" or "Harder"			
Problem	Whites (N = 802)	African Americans (N = 474)	Latinos (N = 252)	Asian Americans (N = 353)
To maintain quality public schools	55	57	45	47
To get good jobs	56	60	50	56
To find decent, affordable housing	55	49	55	48
To stay together as a family	45	48	40	34
To get decent health care	44	39	30	30

Source: Adapted from Jennifer Hochschild and Reuel Rogers, "Race Relations in a Diversifying Nation," in *New Directions: African Americans in a Diversifying Nation*, ed. James Jackson (forthcoming), based on data from the Washington Post/Kaiser Foundation/Harvard Survey Project 1995.

TABLE 2   POLICY PREFERENCES
FOR CONGRESSIONAL ACTION

	Percent Saying "Strongly Feel Congress Should Do"			
Policy Issue	Whites (N = 802)	African Americans (N = 474)	Latinos (N = 252)	Asian Americans (N = 353)
Limit tax breaks for business	39	41	41	30
Balance the budget	82	79	75	75
Cut personal income taxes	52	50	55	46
Reform the welfare system	83	73	81	68
Reform Medicare	53	58	59	58
Put more limits on abortion	35	32	50	24
Limit affirmative action	38	25	30	27

Source: Adapted from Jennifer Hochschild and Reuel Rogers, "Race Relations in a Diversifying Nation," in *New Directions: African Americans in a Diversifying Nation*, ed. James Jackson (forthcoming), based on data from the Washington Post/Kaiser Foundation/Harvard Survey Project 1995.

strong preferences for congressional action—with overwhelming support for balancing the budget and changing the welfare system, less enthusiasm for cutting personal income taxes and reforming Medicare, and even less for business tax breaks. Finally, as Jennifer Hochschild and Reuel Rogers point out, there is considerable convergence in views across racial and ethnic groups with regard to policy preferences for solving particular problems, including education, crime, gang violence, and drugs.[18]

The development and articulation of an ideological vision that captures and highlights commonalities in basic core values and attitudes is paramount in establishing the case for a progressive multiracial political coalition and defusing the opposition of pessimists who promote the more limited advantages of group-specific political mobilization.[19]*

Social psychological research on interdependence reveals that when people believe that they need each other they relinquish

*However, Lani Guinier and Gerald Torres argue that the most effective way to involve minorities in racially inclusive coalitions is to organize them first around political issues that are explicitly race-specific. They assert that racial minorities are less likely to respond to calls for coalition building if their leaders do not first speak to and organize them around matters that relate to their racial experiences. Only then, it is argued, would it be possible to get racial minorities to expand their concerns and embrace issues that interest all groups. This claim is reasonable, but there is little systematic evidence to support it. Indeed, none of the successful multiracial coalitions discussed later in this chapter used this two-step process of minority involvement. (See Lani Guinier and Gerald Torres, "Critical Race Theory Revisited," the second of three Nathan I. Huggins Lectures, Harvard University, Cambridge, Massachusetts, April 20, 1999.)

their initial prejudices and stereotypes and join programs that foster mutual interaction and cooperation. Moreover, when people from different groups do get along, their perceptions about and behavior toward each other undergo change.[20] Under such circumstances, not only are efforts made by the participants in the research experiment to behave in ways that do not disrupt the interaction, but they also make an effort to express consistent and similar attitudes and opinions about an issue that confronts and concerns them.[21]

These conclusions are based mainly on David W. Johnson, Roger Johnson, and Geoffrey Maruyama's review and analysis of ninety-eight experimental studies of goal interdependence and interpersonal attraction. They revealed support in the research literature for the idea that interpersonal attraction among different racial and ethnic groups is enhanced by cooperative experiences. One reason for enhanced cooperation is that "within cooperative situations participants benefit from encouraging others to achieve, whereas in competitive situations participants benefit from obstructing others' efforts to achieve."[22] Accordingly, promotive interaction is greater within situations that are cooperative than in those that are competitive. The research reported considerably more interaction across ethnic lines in cooperative situations, and more cross-ethnic helping in such situations as well. In addition, the research indicated that cooperative situations enhance *social perspective taking*, "the ability to understand how a situation appears to another person and how that person is reacting cognitively and emotionally to it."[23] Finally, the research revealed that within cooperative situations "participants seemed to have a differentiated view of collaborators and tended to minimize perceived differences in ability and view all collaborators as being equally worthwhile, regardless of their performance level or ability."[24]

This research suggests the need for effective leadership to develop and articulate an ideological vision that not only highlights common interests, norms, values, aspirations, and goals, but also helps individuals and groups appreciate the importance of interracial cooperation to achieve and sustain them. This does not mean that group differences are not acknowledged in this vision. As the Harvard sociologist Marshall Ganz has pointed out, "acknowledging differences is essential to collaborating around common interest. . . . It is important not to pretend that we are all the same." He notes that racial and ethnic groups have important differences, "but these become resources rather than liabilities if we come up with ways to [build] on our commonalities."[25]

Visionary group leaders, especially those who head strong community organizations, are essential for articulating and communicating this vision, as well as for developing and sustaining this multiracial political coalition. According to the political scientist Raphael J. Sonenshein, the most effective coalitions are those that begin building in communities with strong political organizations already in place.[26]

Nonetheless, there is a common perception that given America's history of racial division and its current racism, it is naive to assume that a national multiracial coalition with a mass-based economic agenda could ever materialize. Many who share this perception do not consider seriously the possibility of creating the conditions of perceived interdependence needed to promote interracial cooperation and coalition building. Nor do they entertain the idea that given the right social circumstances, including the presence of creative, visionary leaders, such conditions could emerge.

However, there are cases from historical and contemporary America that cast doubt on such pessimism. A comprehensive study of interracial unionism during the Great Depression, for example, reveals that the United Auto Workers in Detroit, the primarily Pennsylvania-based Steel Workers Organizing Committee, and the similarly based United Mine Workers were "able to organize a racially mixed labor force in settings where past racial antagonisms and minority strike-breaking had been sources of labor defeat."[27] The interracial solidarity was facilitated by a number of factors that relate to general principles about perceived interdependence and that represent structural conditions conducive to interracial cooperation. These factors include racial convergence of orientations toward the labor market, a favorable political context featuring legislation (for example, the Wagner Act) that facilitated organizing activities, and changes in organizing tactics "that institutionalize racial inclusiveness in the union structure."[28]

Moreover, multiracial grassroots community organizations whose institutions, actions, and belief systems exemplify the very conditions of perceived interdependence do in fact exist today in this country. These groups benefit from the presence of forward-looking leaders who have effectively mobilized groups in their communities to achieve local goals. A notable example is the Living Wage Campaign. In a number of cities coalitions of local labor leaders, community-based organizations, religious leaders, and student groups, with multiracial participation, have prompted the passage of "living wage" ordinances. These ordinances require employers with municipal contracts or subsidies to raise the hourly minimum wage substantially above the federal minimum of $5.15. Living wage campaigns have been successful in sixteen cities, including Baltimore, Boston, Los Angeles, Milwaukee, Minneapolis, and New York. In addition, living wage campaigns are currently underway in seventeen other municipalities, including Albany, Chicago, Denver, Detroit, Philadelphia, Pittsburgh, and St. Louis.

The Living Wage Campaign movement is an excellent example of what can happen when local leaders are able to forge coalitions to rally behind an issue that concerns all races, in this case economic justice. With direct access to city legislators, leaders of these coalitions have been able to demonstrate the importance of mutual cooperation in achieving desired political goals.

The movement's first victory was in Baltimore in 1997, when a living wage ordinance was passed that required contractors doing business with the city to pay their workers a minimum of $6.10 an hour. Today they must pay $7.70 an hour, which is indexed to the rate of inflation. Los Angeles requires companies doing business with the city to pay a minimum wage of $7.25 an hour plus health benefits and twelve days of paid vacation. The city council in San Jose recently passed the highest living wage ordinance in the country, requiring businesses that receive city service contracts to pay their workers a minimum of $9.50 an hour with health benefits, or $10.75 an hour if employees do not receive health benefits. Reflecting on this legislation, Harry Kelber of *Sweat Labor Magazine* writes: "Although living-wage ordinances are limited to workers whose employers have contracts or other economic relationships with the city, they will put pressure on other employers to upgrade the wages of their workers."[29]

The Living Wage Campaign is gaining momentum, and whether it will expand to embrace other issues of economic and social justice remains to be seen. If it does, perhaps it might benefit from the lessons and experiences of a longer standing and very effective multiracial political coalition at the local level— namely, the national community organization networks of the Industrial Areas Foundation.[30]

A Case Study of an Effective Multiracial Political Coalition at the Grassroots Level: The Industrial Areas Foundation

More than fifty years ago, Saul Alinsky founded the Industrial Areas Foundation in conjunction with his efforts to organize Chicago's marginalized poor. Alinsky envisioned the IAF as a team of professional organizers who could identify committed individuals, assemble them for group action, and instruct them in effective methods of community improvement. Through this method, the IAF could help individuals organize into potentially powerful coalitions; IAF professionals could move from place to place in their mission of education and development, while the work of community development and improvement could be carried out by the people with the greatest stake in its success.

Today there is a national network of dynamic IAF organizations in forty communities from California to Massachusetts. To achieve this success, IAF professional organizers have worked within faith-based organizations—in most cases, Christian churches—to identify experienced leaders and to assemble them into nonsectarian coalitions devoted to community development. An important feature of the IAF approach is that even though the members of the coalition are drawn from faith communities, the IAF assembly constitutes an independent organization that is not tied to the participants' respective churches.

IAF organizations are known by many names, such as the Greater Boston Interfaith Organization (GBIO), Tying Nashville Together (TNT), East Brooklyn Churches (EBC), Baltimoreans United in Leadership Development (BUILD), and Valley Organized Community Efforts (VOICE), in Los Angeles County. Each organization reflects the distinctive needs of its community, because the agenda of each is determined by its leaders and members, not by the IAF.

Some of the IAF's most successful organizations are in Texas, where eleven IAF institutions are active across the state. Included among these is the San Antonio–based Communities Organized for Public Service (COPS), the largest, longest-standing IAF institution in the country and generally regarded as one of the strongest community organizations in the nation. COPS initiatives have resulted in hundreds of millions of dollars of infrastructure improvements in poor inner-city neighborhoods of San Antonio, through the upgrading or repair of streets, sidewalks, public lighting, and sewer drainage and the establishment or construction of parks and libraries. In addition, COPS has been responsible for the construction or rehabilitation of thousands of housing units.[31]

In Texas the IAF has created a model statewide network that has effectively influenced political decisions in municipal governments, the state legislature, and the governor's mansion. Furthermore, the network has brought together whites, African Americans, Mexican Americans, Catholics, and Protestants for mutual support in addressing matters of common concern and interest.

In mobilizing leadership in Texas, the IAF has generated and sustained interracial cooperation in three related ways. First, in initially establishing its multiracial organization, the Texas IAF relied on its members' shared commitment to broad religious principles to generate trust and a sense of common identity. Second, Texas IAF issues originate from local consensus and thus are consensual, not divisive; in addition, these issues are always framed in a race-neutral manner. And third, Hispanic, African American, and white leaders are united in local IAF organizations but retain significant autonomy by also serving in other organizations or enterprises that address race- and neighborhood-specific issues that are not part of the Texas IAF agenda, "as long as they remain within the broad unitary framework of the IAF." In other words, members of the IAF are allowed "to participate in race-oriented campaigns separately from their IAF involvement." Thus, the IAF follows a race-neutral strategy, "defining issues in a nonracial manner and emphasizing the potential benefit of its campaigns to all Americans."[32]

Although the IAF has been criticized for not explicitly addressing racial issues,[33] Mark Warren points out that such criticisms "miss the larger significance of the IAF's experience." He goes on to state:

> The IAF does indeed take up very many "issues of race," like poor schools, neighborhood neglect, health care shortages, and lack of economic opportunity. But it frames these issues in nonracial terms, emphasizing the interest of the whole community in addressing them. The IAF follows a local version of universalistic public policy, developing programs potentially open to all but with special benefit to low income, minority communities. . . . The Texas IAF has often proven

adept at redefining issues that many perceive as racial, such
as the poor state of education in inner-city African-American
neighborhoods.[34]

The importance of the IAF's use of religious institutions in
developing and sustaining interracial organizations should not
be underemphasized. The fundamental worldview common to
the Catholic clergy, Protestant ministers, and other active prac-
titioners of Judeo-Christian creeds provides a foundation that allows for trust as its starting point. Seeing their common identity
as "children of God," the leaders of the different racial or ethnic
groups in the Texas IAF more readily perceive the commonality
of their economic and political interests. Working to better the
community for all can be seen as a matter of faith, hope, and
charity. The IAF's consensual political strategy builds on this in-
tersection of faith and action to frame issues within a larger context of religious and family values.[35] "What IAF has found is that
when people learn through politics to work with each other, support one another's projects," claims Ernesto Cortes (head of the
Southwest IAF), "a trust emerges that goes beyond the barriers
of race, ethnicity, income, and geography; we have found that we
can rebuild community by reconstructing society."[36]

However, as political writer William Greider has argued, in
order to maximize political strength, it is important that a coalition attempt to build bridges not only across the racial divide, but
across the class divide as well. In this connection he points out:

> IAF organizations are already at work on the [class] bridge
> building. Some of the Texas organizations, for instance, are
> truly diverse, with memberships that leap across the usual

lines of race and class. Many white middle-class members, drawn by their Christian or Jewish faith and progressive civic values, have a conscience-driven commitment to their communities and a sense that this is the only politics that produces anything meaningful. . . . Cortes does not think that the IAF Texas network will achieve full status as a major power in the state until it succeeds at creating a presence among the white blue-collar workers in East Texas and elsewhere—people who have common economic interests but are in social conflict with blacks and Hispanics. The organizers are looking for such openings.[37]

In its successes in fostering influential community groups, the IAF provides a model for the development of a multiracial political coalition that would address *national* issues. Recall that social psychological research reveals that people who believe that they need each other go beyond their initial prejudices and stereotypes to join programs that foster mutual interaction and cooperation. And when groups are motivated to get along, their perceptions about and behavior toward each other undergo change. The research indicates that not only does each group make an effort to behave in ways that do not disrupt the interaction, but the groups also make an effort to express consistent and similar attitudes and opinions about an issue that confronts them.

The activities of the IAF support these research findings on mutual group interaction and cooperation. Effective leadership from visionary organizers such as Ernesto Cortes has created an awareness of common interests, goals, and values that can be enhanced by multiracial cooperation. IAF organizations clearly demonstrate that, despite America's strife-ridden racial history, effective leadership can overcome obstacles to foster sustained interracial cooperation. And I believe that IAF groups such as COPS in San Antonio provide a reference point for the proponents of social equality who feel that the development of a multiracial political coalition to address national issues, rather than purely local or regional issues, is feasible and desirable.

A key aspect of IAF successes, however, is also one that garners the groups' major criticism: they do not pursue issues as race-specific problems. Affirmations of racial solidarity are seen as incompatible with the organizations' commitment to build "whenever possible community organizations made up of diverse racial, ethnic and religious groups."[38] For example, in San Antonio, when the Hispanic south and west sides of San Antonio were plagued with floods, the local IAF organization, COPS, did not define the problem as a "Latino issue" or an issue of race; rather, the issue was presented as one of "poor drainage and disgraceful neglect of the lives of citizens of San Antonio."[39] In Fort Worth, Texas, the local IAF's efforts to increase parental involvement in the predominantly African American school were not described in terms of confronting racial discrimination in education; rather, the issue was discussed as one of neglect and failure in the local educational institutions.[40]

In San Antonio, COPS initially fought for improved sidewalks, better drainage systems, and comprehensive street pavings. After succeeding in these pursuits, COPS focused on upgrading housing, improving police protection, pursuing education reform, and promoting economic development. Many of these issues were also effectively pursued by the United Neighborhood Organization (UNO), the IAF chapter in Los Angeles, "along with a successful effort to increase the minimum wage in California."[41] Although both the UNO and COPS are heavily represented by Mexican Americans, issues such as bilingual education and immigration were conspicuously absent from the political agenda.[42] Finally, Texas IAF organizations have not called for municipal affirmative action to increase minority hiring or promotion. Nor have they endorsed political candidates on the basis of their race or ethnicity.[43]

In short, the IAF believes that racially defined issues are divisive and therefore counterproductive.[44] It is possible that defining an issue as a *Latino* issue or as a *black* issue runs the risk of provoking marginalization: if this is a black (Latino) problem, let African American (Mexican American) citizens solve it. But by presenting social and economic problems within the larger framework of support for San Antonio citizens or for Texans (or, given my hope for a nationwide IAF model, even for Americans), IAF-type organizations lay the groundwork for a discussion that shares resources across all groups. And, in fact, although IAF groups are careful to define issues in race-neutral terms, they do address issues of race by confronting the problems of the poor and the overlooked—persons who, in American society, are often racial minorities.

Even though the IAF has been successful in building an effective multiracial coalition by ignoring or avoiding explicit racial issues, would such a strategy be viable in the long run for a national multiracial coalition? If a progressive multiracial coalition is trying to build support for a mass-based economic agenda, a race-neutral strategy makes sense for the most part. Why? Because the goal is to attract wide segments of the population with messages that resonate across racial groups. "Both survey and case study evidence suggests that the more a multiracial coalition focuses on issues of racial and ethnic equality per se, the less stable it will be and the more likely it will be to fragment into competitive factions," state Jennifer Hochschild and Reuel Rogers. "Conversely, the same evidence shows that the more a multiracial coalition focuses on issues that are not ostensibly about race, and that have the potential to involve a wide range of people of all identities, the greater its chance of persistence and success."[45]

However, given the focus on basic economic issues, what about affirmative action? In the context of race-neutral agitation for social change, is affirmative action a divisive, racially explicit issue? Because many Americans view affirmative action programs as central to the continuing quest for economic racial justice in America, can it really be in any multiracial coalition's best interest to exclude such programs from its agenda?

A strategy that avoids explicitly racial issues has not been fatal to the IAF grassroots networks, bound together by a background of religious faith and the work of visionary community leaders who have been able to explain the merits of such a strategy to their constituents. This approach, however, may not work at the national level. For African Americans, affirmative action as national policy is seen as crucial for addressing American racial injustice that ranges from persistent institutional racism to overt racial discrimination. Accordingly, only an extraordinary appeal for a purely race-neutral strategy in employment would attract a significant segment of the black population to the coalition. Just as the coalition is weaker if it cannot attract large segments of the dominant white population, so too is it less powerful if only a fraction of the minority population is involved or interested.

The crucial question, which I address in the following chapter, is this: Is it possible to include affirmative action on the mass-based economic agenda of a multiracial coalition so that it does not become a divisive issue and erode or minimize the support of white citizens?

4

FROM "RACIAL PREFERENCE" TO AFFIRMATIVE OPPORTUNITY

In the face of growing attacks on programs of "racial preference," some analysts, including those who support multiracial
coalition building, have called for a shift from an affirmative action policy based on race to one based on economic class or financial need. In a thoughtful book supporting class-based affirmative action programs, Richard D. Kahlenberg argues that
preferences in hiring or school admissions should benefit only
the economically disadvantaged, regardless of race, ethnicity,
sex, or sexual orientation.[1] For Kahlenberg, only a class-based
affirmative action program would correct society's injustices and
provide genuine individual opportunity. While eliminating benefits for advantaged minorities, it would enhance benefits both for
poor people of color and for poor whites. Moreover, he argues,
class-based affirmative action programs would hasten racial integration, "but without the increased racial prejudice and hostility
associated with racial preferences."[2]

The major distinguishing characteristic of affirmative action based on need is the recognition that the problems of the disadvantaged—low income, crime-ridden neighborhoods, broken homes, inadequate housing, poor education, and cultural and linguistic differences—are not always clearly related to previous racial discrimination. Children who grow up in homes plagued by these disadvantages are more likely to be denied an equal chance in life because the development of their aspirations and talents is hindered by their environment, regardless of race. Proponents of class-based affirmative action programs argue that minorities would benefit disproportionately from affirmative action programs designed to address these disadvantages because they suffer disproportionately from the effects of such environments, but that the problems of disadvantaged whites would be addressed as well.

Yet recent research suggests that class-based affirmative action programs would fail to maintain anywhere near the levels of racial or ethnic diversity attained in the last several years in the nation's leading institutions of higher learning (undergraduate colleges and professional schools) and in professional employment.[3] Class-based policies, however justified, are not a substitute for race-based policies. "Racial differences simply are not reducible to class differences, just as class differences are not reducible to racial ones," states the sociologist Jerome Karabel. "Both race and class are important independent sources of disadvantage in the United States today."[4]

Even after controlling for income, large racial and ethnic differences in Scholastic Aptitude Test (SAT) scores remain. And the racial gap in SAT scores is largest among the very group who would be targeted for a class-based affirmative action program—low-income students. Data from California illustrate an important fact. The differential in SAT scores between white and Mexican American students is 91 points for those with family incomes above $60,000 a year, but the gap increases to 188 points for those with family incomes below $20,000 a year. Data from the same study suggest that low-income white and Asian Americans would be the primary beneficiaries of class-based affirmative action programs. "Class-based affirmative action is a worthy policy in its own right," states Karabel, "but it will do relatively little to maintain racial and ethnic diversity."[5]

An affirmative action program based solely on financial need or economic class would do little to sustain racial and ethnic diversity, not only because it would produce at best marginal gains in the college enrollment of lower-income blacks and Hispanics, but also because it would result in the systematic exclusion of many middle-income blacks (as well as middle-income Hispanics) from desirable positions. Why? Because the standard or conventional measures of performance are not sensitive to the cumulative effects of race or ethnicity. By this I mean having one's life choices restricted by race, regardless of class, because of the effects of living in segregated neighborhoods (that is, being exposed to styles of behavior, habits, and the particular skills that emerge from patterns of racial exclusion), because of the quality of de facto segregated schooling, and because of nurturing by parents whose experiences have also been shaped and limited by race, which ultimately affects the resources they are able to pass on to their children.

A number of empirical studies have revealed significant differences in the family and neighborhood environments of blacks and whites that are understated when standard measures of socioeconomic status (SES) are employed.[6] Take, for example, the question of family environment. Even when white and black parents report the same average income, white parents have substantially more assets than do black parents.[7] Whites with the same amount of schooling as blacks usually attend better high schools and colleges. Furthermore, children's test scores are affected not only by the SES of their parents, but also by the SES of their grandparents. This means that it could take several generations before adjustments in socioeconomic inequality produce their full benefits.[8]

When we speak of reducing social inequality, we often lose sight of or fail to capture the impact of organizational and collective processes that embody the social structure of inequality and have varied influences on different racial and ethnic groups. Among these processes are the institutional influences on mobility and opportunity, including activities of employers' associations and labor unions; the operation and organization of schools; the mechanisms of residential racial segregation and social isolation in poor neighborhoods; categorical forms of discrimination in hiring, promotion, and other work-related matters; ideologies of group differences shared by members of society and institutionalized in organizational practices and norms that affect social outcomes; and differential racial and ethnic group access to information concerning the labor market, financial markets, education and training, schools, and so on.[9]

Thus, if we were to rely solely on the standard criteria for college admission, such as SAT scores, even many children from

African American and Hispanic middle-income families would be denied admission in favor of middle-income whites. The latter are not weighed down by the accumulation of disadvantages that stem from racial or ethnic restrictions and therefore tend to score higher on these conventional measures.

Affirmative action based solely on need or economic class position could create a situation in which a few African Americans and Hispanics from low-income families would be admitted to highly selective and elite institutions of higher learning, whereas those from middle-income families would tend to be excluded because they would not be eligible for consideration under class-based affirmative action guidelines. They would therefore be left to compete in a race-blind admissions policy with middle- and upper-income whites whose test scores and life experiences are not limited by the handicaps of race.

As Nathan Glazer has recently pointed out, the Harvards, the Berkeleys, and the Amhersts "have become, for better or worse, the gateways to prominence, privilege, wealth, and power in American society." To exclude large segments of the minority population from these institutions by abolishing race-based affirmative action "would undermine the legitimacy of American democracy."[10]

We only need to examine the results of aptitude tests for college and professional school admission to gauge the effects of abolishing race-based affirmative action programs. In the nation's top twenty-five institutions of higher learning, the average combined SAT (verbal and math) score for entering freshmen is roughly 1300. Less than 2 percent of black students nationwide attain this score.[11] With the elimination of affirmative action admission practices at the University of California, projections of college enrollments at Berkeley and UCLA suggest that the proportion of historically underrepresented minorities will plummet perhaps by one-half over the next several years.[12]

In 1996 fewer than one in ten of the California students who scored over 600 in each of the verbal and math sections of the SAT (for a combined score over 1200) were either black or Latino. And of those who scored over 700 in each of these sections of the exam, the combined black-Latino proportion was 6 percent in the verbal and less than 4 percent in the math.[13] It is not surprising therefore that the university's mandated race-blind policies resulted in a substantial decline in black and Latino college admission at the highly selective universities. The admission of underrepresented minorities dropped 61 percent at Berkeley in 1998. However, because of a more comprehensive approach to admissions—including the consideration of parental income and education levels, the student's comparison with others in high school, and the proportion of honors courses taken among those that were offered—Berkeley admitted 29 percent more underrepresented minorities in the fall of 1999 than in the fall of 1998. Nonetheless, this 1999 rate is still far below the rates of underrepresented minority admissions during the years prior to the adoption of the University of California's anti-affirmative action measure.[14]

Race-blind admissions policies have produced similar sharp declines in professional schools. Following the passage of Proposition 209, the anti-affirmative action initiative, only 15 African American students were admitted to the University of California's Law School in Berkeley, down from 75 in 1996. And only 11 blacks were admitted to the University of Texas Law School in

1997 after the U.S. Court of Appeals struck down that school's affirmative action program; this was a dramatic change from the admission of 65 black students the previous year.[15]

The admission of minority students with lower SAT scores to selective institutions of higher learning has prompted a frequent charge against racial preference policies. Critics say that such policies harm the intended beneficiaries because they entice young people to attend institutions for which they are insufficiently prepared, which causes them to face competition they cannot handle.[16] However, the evidence does not support such assumptions. Even after holding constant an individual's academic preparation and family background, a study by the economist Thomas J. Kane, based on the High School and Beyond Surveys (HSB) from 1982 to 1992, revealed that for the class of 1982, higher four-year degree completion rates and higher earnings were associated with attending a more selective college for all students, minority and otherwise. Preexisting differences in academic potential do correlate with some of the differences in college completion rates and earnings between minorities and whites, but, as Kane points out, "there is no evidence in the HSB data to suggest that black and Hispanic students benefit less than others from attending a selective college."[17]

Moreover, there is reason to question the use of selection criteria in college admissions that rely heavily on conventional aptitude tests. Indeed, it is not readily apparent to what extent standard aptitude tests like the SAT or the Law School Admission Test (LSAT)—even tests used for promoting police officers—measure real merit or potential to succeed rather than privilege. The research reveals that for most applicants, these tests are only tenuously related to future performance. They "tell us more about past opportunity than about future accomplishments on the job or in the classroom."[18] Recent studies show a weak relationship between test scores and job performance.[19] In one study only 9 percent of the variation in predicted job performance was accounted for by the standard aptitude test.[20] And studies at the University of Pennsylvania Law School and the University of Texas Law School found weak correlations between LSAT scores and law school performance.[21]

Ideally, we should develop *flexible, merit-based* criteria of evaluation (or performance measures), as opposed to numerical guidelines or quotas, that would not exclude people with background handicaps, including minority racial ones. These more flexible measures would identify applicants with handicaps who have as much potential to succeed as those without handicaps. Although some test scores may correlate with future performance, they do not necessarily measure other important attributes such as perseverance, motivation, interpersonal skills, reliability, and leadership qualities.[22]

If you compare an inner-city youngster from the ghettos of Roxbury in Boston (or Harlem in New York, Woodlawn in Chicago, or East St. Louis in southern Illinois) who displays these traits and a youngster from white suburbia who has a higher SAT score but does not possess these traits, the chances are good that the inner-city youngster will experience a higher level of college achievement. In the words of Susan Sturm and Lani Guinier, we need to "improve the capacity of institutions to find people who are creative, adaptive, reliable, and committed, rather than just good at test-taking."[23]

The idea of flexible, merit-based criteria does not mean that standard aptitude tests such as the SAT should be abandoned; rather, they should be given less weight in the decision-making process surrounding school admissions. For example, a college admissions committee may recognize and take into account the fact that high school grades consistently predict college freshman grades more accurately than the SAT in both selective and nonselective colleges. And little predictive power is gained by combining the SAT with high school grades.[24] Questions about the predictive power of cognitive tests have also been raised in the employment context, where there is a growing awareness of the value of alternative screening devices such as interviews, job experience, education, and peer evaluations.[25]

The obvious rejoinder from critics of affirmative action programs is that "using flexible criteria" is another way of saying that lower standards will be tolerated. On the contrary, using flexible criteria of evaluation will ensure that we are measuring merit or potential to succeed rather than privilege. In other words, we want to use criteria that will not exclude people who have as much potential to succeed as those from more privileged backgrounds.

The differences in average test scores touted by some opponents of affirmative action are largely measures of differences in opportunities between the advantaged and the disadvantaged, especially factors early in life such as access to high quality child care and good schooling. Research reviewed in a recent article by Sturm and Guinier "indicates that many tests correlate quite closely with parental income. . . . The correlation between family income and SAT is nearly four times larger than the incremental improvement in prediction offered by the SAT used in conjunction with high school grades. In other words, the SAT, at the margins, is a better predictor of family income than of first-year college grades."[26]

The advantages of family income are seen in the differential access of children from lower- and higher-income families to courses on the art of test taking.[27] White undergraduates, whose families on average have higher incomes than those of black undergraduates, more frequently pay the $1,000 fee to take LSAT prep courses offered by several test preparation companies. Some observers feel that increasing black access to LSAT prep courses would be an effective short-term effort to increase the number of competitive minorities. According to one recent report, only "28% of blacks had taken a prep course, compared with 37% of whites and about 36% of Asians."[28] Although this difference is not large, it obscures another disparity: African American students are clustered in the less expensive and less intensive weekend prep courses.[29]

Thus, as Sturm and Guinier appropriately point out, "what is often touted as a merit-based standard is instead arbitrary and exclusionary. It is arbitrary when it does not correlate well with what it is supposed to be measuring. It is exclusionary when test scores often correlate reliably with parental income. Test scores tell us more about the past than the future."[30]

Flexible criteria accommodate the need to design metrics of ability that predict success but are not captured by such tests. Indications of these attributes may be obtained from letters of recommendation, past performance, or other measures. Mayor Richard Daley's use of "merit promotions" in the Chicago police department is based on such factors as job performance and leadership ability and constitutes an example of how such criteria can be used.

Relying on flexible, merit-based criteria may be a way of replacing the goals and timetables currently used by government
agencies. Having said that, I should note that it will be extremely
important to calibrate the use of flexible criteria in practice.
They must be presented as a way of expanding the pool of qualified applicants by making attributes other than raw test scores
count more. Flexible criteria must be applied in thoughtful ways,
based on the experience of what works in certain situations and
institutions.

Let me briefly discuss two case studies that illustrate the effective use of flexible criteria of evaluation—at the University of
California, Irvine, and the University of Michigan Law School.
In response to the vote of the University of California's regents
to eliminate affirmative action in admissions, the University of
California, Irvine, developed and implemented "admissions criteria consistent with the new guidelines."[31] Although test scores
and other standard criteria such as grades and courses completed
remain important elements in the selection process, additional
factors are considered significant components based on the assumption that "merit is demonstrated in many forms and measured in different ways."[32] These factors include such criteria as
an applicant's initiative and leadership, ability to overcome personal hardship, self-awareness ("that is, evidence of active commitment based on self-identified values"), civic and cultural
awareness, honors and awards, and specialized knowledge.[33]

The selection of some of these criteria was based on involvement theory, which emphasizes that "students who become so-
cialized and involved in their education are more likely to succeed."[34] In order to determine the impact of the new admission
process instituted in fall 1997, Susan Wilbur and Marguerite

Bonous-Hammarth "compared the actual makeup of the newly admitted freshman class with the hypothetical makeup of a class admitted solely on the basis . . . of a ranking system based on the GPA and test scores." The comparison revealed that the use of more flexible criteria at the University of California, Irvine, "resulted in significant gains for underrepresented ethnic groups—particularly African Americans, American Indians, and Chicanos," whose admission rates increased respectively by 30 percent, 24 percent, and 21 percent.[35]*

The University of Michigan Law School Admissions Office provides another example of the effective use of flexible, merit-based criteria. Ironically, the University of Michigan Law School faces an anti-affirmative action lawsuit challenging the denial of admission to a white applicant, Ms. Barbara Grutter. She claims that she was denied admission in favor of less qualified minority applicants. This court suit follows on the heels of the recent decision of the U.S. Court of Appeals for the Fifth Circuit in *Hopwood v. Texas*. That decision struck down the University of Texas Law School's affirmative action program, which set numerical goals to increase the enrollment of underrepresented groups (African Americans, Latinos, women, and so on). The goals were established by determining the proportion of underrepresented groups in the applicant pool.[36]

*However, Wilbur and Bonous-Hammarth point out that "even under the old, more formulaic system, UCI did not admit students only on the basis of grade point averages and test scores. Other information, like honors and awards, was given some consideration. Nevertheless, this preliminary analysis offers a gross comparison that is useful."

However, unlike the University of Texas Law School's affirmative action program, the University of Michigan's program is not based on racial quotas or numerical guidelines. As Jeffrey S. Lehman, dean of the University of Michigan Law School, put it:

> We are confident that our admissions policy is constitutional. It conforms to the requirements of the Fourteenth Amendment as set forth in Justice Powell's opinion in *Regents of the University of California v. Bakke*. Our admissions office does not use racial quotas. The percentage of students of different races in our entering classes vary noticeably from year to year. We use diversity as a factor within the larger context of our policy of admitting only students whom we expect to go on to become outstanding lawyers.[37]

In addition to an index score that represents an applicant's grade point average and LSAT score, the University of Michigan Law School Admissions Office relies heavily on a number of other factors in judging each applicant. Included among these are letters of recommendation, the application essay, the quality of the applicant's undergraduate institution, the areas of difficulty in undergraduate course selection, personal experiences or perspectives likely to contribute to a diverse student body, and evidence of leadership ability. As stated in the *Report and Recommendation of the Admission Committee,*

> Many qualities not captured in grades and test scores figure in the evaluation of an applicant. . . . Precisely which characteristics should be valued is a matter left to the Dean of Admissions and the Admissions Committee. . . . No doubt the kinds of conditions that make for valued diversity will change

to some degree each year as the composition of the admissions committee changes. The varied perspectives from which different committees will interpret the concept of "diversity" should further enrich our school.[38]

The point to be emphasized is that the number of minority applicants admitted to the University of Michigan Law School varies each year, dependent on the strength of their applications. No numerical guidelines or quotas are set. The use of these flexible criteria has resulted in an outstanding number of minority law school students over the past several years.[39]

Would an emphasis on flexible, merit-based criteria of evaluation help to overcome the widespread opposition to affirmative action programs, so that such programs could be firmly institutionalized in this country? Nathan Glazer indicates that, despite complaints about affirmative action from the majority of citizens, "there was (and is) no major elite constituency strongly opposed to it; neither business nor organized labor, religious leaders nor university presidents, local officials nor serious presidential candidates are to be found in opposition." Glazer adds that "big business used to fear that affirmative action would undermine the principle of employment and promotion on the basis of qualifications. It has since become a supporter. Along with mayors and other local officials (and of course the civil rights movement), it played a key role in stopping the Reagan administration from moving against affirmative action."[40]*

*As Jennifer L. Hochschild has pointed out: "Opponents of affirmative action have found to their surprise and disgust that their apparent allies in the conservative business community either reject or politely distance themselves from political efforts to abolish affirmative action.

Nonetheless, despite a slight decrease in opposition to affirmative action programs in education and employment between 1986 and 1990, sentiment against these programs among the general public remains strong. In 1990 almost seven in ten white Americans opposed quotas to admit black students in colleges and universities, and more than eight in ten objected to the idea of preferential hiring and promotion of blacks.

However, such strong white opposition to quotas and preferential hiring and promotion should not lead us to overlook the fact that some affirmative action policies are supported by wide segments of the white population, regardless of racial attitudes. As the Harvard sociologist Lawrence Bobo has recently pointed out, the view that white opposition to affirmative action is monolithic is distorted. "Affirmative action policies span a range of

---

California's Proposition 209 was funded largely by the Republican Party and individual Republican political actors. Corporations such as Shell Oil Company, Boeing Corporation, Nordstrom's, and Pacific Gas and Electric Company opposed it. Proposition A in Houston was funded mostly by the leader of the initiative and the American Civil Rights Coalition, the Houston Chamber of Commerce opposed it, Boeing, Weyerhauser, and Microsoft opposed the proposition in the state of Washington, and Nordstrom's remained neutral. No major corporation in the state supported it. Thus, although corporations will continue to defend themselves against claims of discrimination, and although it will be a long time—if ever—before corporate leadership resembles the American, racial, ethnic, or gender structures, it nevertheless is safe to predict that most corporations will not actively support measures to abolish affirmative action in the states or in Congress" (Jennifer L. Hochschild, "The Strange Career of Affirmative Action," *Ohio State Law Review* 59 [winter 1999]: 1017–18).

policy goals and strategies. Some formulations of which (e.g., race-targeted scholarships or special job outreach and training efforts) can be quite popular."[41] For example, recent studies reveal that, although they oppose such "preferential" racial policies as college admission quotas or job hiring and promotion strategies designed to achieve equal outcomes, most white Americans approve of such "opportunity-enhancing" affirmative action policies as race-targeted programs for job training, special education, and recruitment. In the 1990 General Social Survey, 68 percent of all whites favored spending more money on schools in black neighborhoods, especially for preschool and early education programs. And 70 percent favored granting special college scholarships to black children who maintain good grades.[42] In their large survey of households in the Boston metropolitan area, Barry Bluestone and Mary Huff Stevenson found that whereas only 18 percent of the white male and 13 percent of the white female respondents favored or strongly favored job *preferences* for blacks, 59 percent of the white males and 70 percent of the white females favored or strongly favored special job training and education for blacks.[43]

Accordingly, programs that enable blacks to take advantage of opportunities, such as race-targeted early education programs, job training, and college scholarships that reward academic achievement, are less likely to be "perceived as challenging the values of individualism and the work ethic."[44] In other words, opportunity-enhancing affirmative action programs are supported because they reinforce the belief that the allocation of jobs and economic rewards should be based on individual effort, training, and talent.

Affirmative Opportunity

Unlike "preferential" racial policies, opportunity-enhancing programs have popular support even among those who express antiblack attitudes. For all these reasons, *to make the most effective case for affirmative action programs in a period when such programs are under attack from many quarters, emphasis should be shifted from numerical guidelines to opportunity.* The concept I would use to signal this shift is *affirmative opportunity*. By substituting the word *opportunity* for *action*, the concept draws the focus away from a guarantee of equal results, which is how affirmative action has come to be understood. It echoes the phrase *equal opportunity*, which connotes a principle that most Americans still support, while avoiding connotations now associated (fairly or not) with the idea of affirmative action—connotations such as quotas, lowering standards, and reverse discrimination, which most Americans detest.*

By retaining the term *affirmative*, the concept keeps the connotation that something more than formal, legal equality is

---

*The idea of "affirmative opportunity" was outlined in my Aaron Wildavsky lecture delivered at the University of California, Berkeley in April 1996. Since then Glenn Loury and Carol M. Swain have developed similar ideas. In spelling out their arguments, Loury uses the concept "developmental affirmative action" and Swain proffers the concept "soft" affirmative action. (See Glenn C. Loury, "How to Mend Affirmative Action," *The Public Interest* [spring 1997]: 33–43, and "Absolute California: Can the Golden State Go Color-Blind?" *The New Republic*, November 18, 1996, pp. 17–20; and Carol M. Swain, "Affirmative Action: A Search for Consensus" [paper presented at the National Academy of Sciences, Research Conference on Racial Trends in the United States, Washington D.C., October 15, 1998].)

required to overcome the legacy of slavery and Jim Crow segregation. As a society, we have the continuing moral obligation to compensate for the enduring burdens—the social and psychological damage—of segregation, discrimination, and bigotry. *Affirmative opportunity* means to renew the nation's commitment to enable all Americans, regardless of income, race, or other attributes, to achieve the highest level that their abilities permit.

Research on procedural fairness suggests that the ideas of flexible, merit-based criteria of evaluation and affirmative opportunity would resonate with the general public. In one national survey the political scientist Carol M. Swain found that a majority of the respondents, black and white alike, supported a conceptualization of merit that was not restricted to the performance and proficiency level attained by the student. In addition to the standard questionnaire format, this survey included vignettes designed to elicit information about college admission criteria and views on performance versus seniority in situations involving employment and promotion. These vignettes did not include code words such as *preferential treatment*.

Swain reports that the respondents felt that in the college admissions process consideration should be given to obstacles or hardships that a student had to overcome. In other words, colleges ought to consider a student's potential on the basis of his or her successful navigation of difficult circumstances in, say, high-risk environments. Though responses to questions in the larger survey reveal a clear rejection of the idea that racial preferences should guide admission decisions, these respondents seem "to be asking [university admissions officers] to take into consideration more factors than academic preparation alone."[45]

Another study shows that support for affirmative action shifts depending on how the policy is implemented. In this study college students were presented with various affirmative action policies, and their support for these plans varied dramatically depending on how the policies were framed. The respondents strongly disapproved of the race-proportional hiring of *unqualified* candidates, but approved of the race-proportional hiring of candidates who were *qualified* for the position.[46] Support for this particular wording of affirmative action policies comes not only from female and minority respondents, but from white males as well. In other words, even those who would receive no gain from supporting any kind of affirmative action were willing to back a plan that reflects procedural fairness. Finally, another study, based on telephone interviews with a random sample of residents in the San Francisco Bay area, demonstrated that support for affirmative action policies varied according to judgments about the fairness of the policy, regardless of the effect of the policy on the interviewee's individual or group interest.[47]

As Carol M. Swain concludes, "The majority of Americans, both white and black alike, are not enthusiastic about racial preference programs, but can agree on some affirmative action-related issues once we move beyond the racially inflammatory code words found all too often in existing surveys."[48] We only need to be reminded that if the opponents to affirmative action in Houston, Texas, had been able to adopt the language used in Proposition 209 in California and in Initiative Measure 200 in the state of Washington—language that included the term *preferential treatment*—their proposal to abolish municipal-sponsored affirmative action programs would probably have passed, as the public opinion polls in Houston clearly suggested.*

As Jerome Karabel reminds us, it is true that Americans worry about quotas and about "unqualified" people being hired, promoted, and admitted to colleges and universities, but they also recognize "that the playing field is not level and that programs are needed to ensure equal opportunities for minorities and women."[49] That argument probably explains why, following President Clinton's 1995 speech on affirmative action, two national opinion polls, despite slightly different wording, found that 60 to 65 percent of American voters approved of the president's position that affirmative action should be mended and not ended.[50]

I strongly agree with Susan Sturm and Lani Guinier that proponents of affirmative action need "to reclaim the moral high ground . . . and broaden and expand the terms of engagement." Faulty assumptions about both the concept of affirmative action and its system of selection need to be revealed, they argue. "Certainly, we must challenge out loud the basic assumption that affirmative action is a departure from an otherwise sound meritocracy."[51]

*Initiative Measure 200 in the state of Washington read: "Shall government be prohibited from discriminating or granting preferential treatment based on race, sex, color, ethnicity or national origin in public employment, education, and contracting?" It was supported by a majority of Washington voters on November 3, 1998. Proposition 209 in California used almost identical language and was deceptively titled the California Civil Rights Initiative.

Affirmative Opportunity and the
Multiracial Political Coalition

In the previous chapter I pointed out that one reason why the IAF avoids addressing race-explicit issues like affirmative action is that such issues are divisive and ultimately undermine the consensus needed to sustain multiracial cooperation. However, I suggested that it would be problematic in practical terms for a national multiracial coalition to take the same approach. Why? Mainly because it would need to attract the support of a significant segment of the minority population, particularly the African American community.

African Americans see a national affirmative action policy as crucial for addressing American racial injustice. Only an extraordinary appeal for a purely race-neutral strategy would attract a significant segment of the black population to the coalition. Accordingly, the appropriate question is not whether the coalition should ignore the issue of affirmative action. The appropriate question is whether the issue can be framed as part of the broader political agenda designed to benefit all Americans.

Considering the arguments in the foregoing sections, we can assume that if the leaders of the coalition were to emphasize the idea of affirmative opportunity, as opposed to numerical guidelines or quotas, they would have a nondivisive strategy to enhance minority economic mobility. As I have noted, support for affirmative action policies varies according to judgments about the fairness of the policy, regardless of the extent to which the policy affects an individual's own or group interest.

On the basis of the available research, the leaders of such a coalition would be wise to promote not only the idea of procedural fairness when pursuing programs of affirmative opportunity, but also the need for a level playing field to ensure equal opportunities for minorities and women. Moreover, they should turn away from numerical guidelines or quotas and highlight instead the use of flexible, merit-based criteria of evaluation to enlarge the pool of eligible candidates.

Affirmative opportunity programs remain vital to a progressive strategy and central to the continuing quest for racial justice in America. By changing the language we use when discussing such programs, we increase their potential for public support and make them acceptable as an important part of a progressive multiracial coalition's agenda to fight social inequality in the American economy.

5

BRIDGING THE RACIAL DIVIDE AND COALITION POLITICS

Adequate political solutions to the global economic problems confronting the majority of Americans will not be found until white, black, Latino, Asian, and Native Americans begin thinking more about what they have in common and less about their differences. In order to clear the path for the formation of a national, progressive, multiracial political coalition, proponents of social equality must pursue policies that unite rather than divide racial groups.

The idea that diverse racial groups can work together to pursue mutual goals is not taken seriously by many Americans because of the perception that racial friction is an unavoidable fact of American life. This message is transmitted in many ways, including demagogic propaganda designed to generate white anger at racial minorities and the government. Although the most virulent forms of racial ideology have all but disappeared in American society, milder forms of cultural racist ideology, as I describe in chapter 1, persist, whereby whites feel that African

Americans are mainly responsible for their own inferior economic position and are therefore undeserving of government assistance.

Yet at any given point in time, racial ideology, however widely endorsed, can be strengthened or weakened by social, economic, and political situations. Accordingly, if the goal is to overcome obstacles to the creation of multiracial coalitions, then our focus should not be on existing racial ideology, but on the societal conditions that encourage it to flourish or allow it to subside.

From the early 1970s through the first half of the 1990s, economic trends that increased income inequality—including the decline of real wages for a substantial portion of American families—caused ordinary American families to feel economically pinched; many were barely able to maintain current standards of living even on two incomes. During periods of economic anxiety, citizens become more receptive to simplistic ideological messages that deflect attention away from the real sources of their problems, and these periods of economic difficulty provide ideologues an opportunity to promote antagonistic attitudes about race. In recent years, particularly during the first half of the 1990s, these messages, featuring the milder—cultural—form of racist ideology, increased voter resentment and anger against minorities and the government.

Meanwhile, in metropolitan areas, the decline of the central city continued apace of an increase in racial tensions. As cities lost population to the suburbs they became poorer and darker, which in turn promoted a steady decline in their political influence and provided the foundation for the New Federalism. As federal and state governments turned away from sponsoring urban programs, municipalities relied more on local taxes. But as wealth and economic development shifted increasingly to the suburbs, many city governments experienced difficulty raising sufficient revenue from local sources and therefore had to cut basic services. This downward trend reinforced the reluctance of businesses to invest in central-city areas, and the declining quality of urban life prompted even more city residents to move to outlying metropolitan areas.

The current cleavage between the central city and the suburbs is in many ways a racial divide. After all, three-quarters of the dominant white population now lives in suburban and rural areas, whereas a majority of blacks and Latinos reside in urban areas. Although the financial health of many urban areas has improved in the last few years as a result of the recent economic recovery, the city is viewed by many as a less desirable place in which to live, and the demographic, social, and economic gap between cities and suburbs continues to grow. Within cities themselves, remaining groups compete for limited resources, which heightens racial tension.

Throughout the first half of the 1990s, racial demagoguery that placed the economic woes of the country on the shoulders of welfare queens, affirmative action employment policies, and recent immigrants rather than on global markets and industrial restructuring became increasingly strident, until it dominated much of the public discussion around the 1994 congressional election. Thankfully, since 1996 the intensity and frequency of divisive messages have subsided noticeably—no doubt, because the national economy has improved. I believe that this improved economic and social climate sets the stage for meaningful change, and I look to the proponents of multiracial coalitions to seize this opportunity and build on this shift in the public mood.

To strengthen the foundation for multiracial cooperation, we need to develop a new public dialogue on how our problems should be defined and how they should be addressed. This public dialogue should feature a rhetoric that focuses on problems that plague broad segments of the American public—from the jobless poor to the struggling working and middle classes—and emphasizes integrative programs that would promote the social and economic well-being of all these different groups.

A century ago, as Richard Parker reminds us, progressive thinkers focused their attention on two, often overlapping, groups—the poor and the working class, usually described as simply "the working class." In the eyes of these progressives the identity of the working class was distinct not only from the capitalists, but from the then somewhat small middle class as well. More recently, in a period during which labor unions have lost much of their power, the poor, as distinct from the working class, has been the group favored by progressives. "In the sixties, when poverty was 'rediscovered,'" states Parker, "the war against it focused heavily on race and regions (the South and inner cities), on the unemployed or marginally employed—in such a way that, as the Reagan years painfully taught us, a major political gulf opened between, on the one side middle-class and blue-collar voters and, on the other, the Democrats and progressive politics generally." What is needed, argues Parker, is a progressive politics that affirms "that we are also for the much larger middle class and want to see it prosper."[1] I fully agree.

We also need to develop a vocabulary that helps ordinary Americans become more aware of how global economic changes as well as monetary, fiscal, and social policies have increased social inequality and how that inequality enhances racial antago-

nisms. And, finally, the public rhetoric should embrace inclusiveness and encourage Americans to remove their racial blinders
and recognize all groups as potential allies in a reform coalition.

Although the various racial groups in America suffer from
many common economic problems, the focus on racial differences obscures that fact for many Americans. This is seen especially in the tendency to view the current economic problems in
the African American community as largely a matter of race. Although blacks still confront racial barriers in the labor market,
many of the problems of low-skilled African American workers
stem from changes in the demand for labor in the global economy. Computerization and the growing internationalization of
economic activity have created a "twist" in the demand for different types of labor in recent years. In general, highly educated
or highly skilled workers have benefited, whereas workers with
lower skills face the growing threat of job displacement and
eroding wages.

Because historic racism has denied equal opportunities in education and training for African Americans, a disproportionate
number of black workers remain unskilled. Accordingly, the decreased relative demand for low-skilled labor has had a greater
impact on blacks than on whites. Nonetheless, low-skilled workers among all racial and ethnic groups have been affected by the
changes in relative demand for labor.

Another problem for workers across racial lines is slow real
wage growth, but the least trained and educated workers have
been hurt the most. Again, because the proportion of low-skilled
African American workers is relatively large, the impact of slow
real wage growth in the U.S. economy is strongly felt in the
black community. Nonetheless, the economic problems in the

black community are often defined solely in racial terms and therefore are viewed as requiring only race-based solutions.

In the African American community, the more black leaders perceive the economic problems in the black community as separate from the national and international trends affecting ordinary American families, the less likely they are to see the need to join forces with other groups to seek economic reform. However, the creation of a progressive multiracial coalition to pursue social policies designed to soften the impact of national and global economic changes on ordinary families should be receiving the highest priority among all leaders committed to eradicating social inequality, including African American leaders.

Indeed, inequality in the labor market has risen just as new constraints have emerged on the use of federal resources to combat social inequities. Moreover, many of the government's actions and policies exacerbate rather than alleviate the economic stresses of ordinary families. I refer to monetary policies that elevate real interest rates and lead to increased unemployment rates, trade policies that place low-skilled labor in the United States in greater competition with low-skilled labor around the world, tax policies that favor the wealthier families at the expense of ordinary families, and congressional inaction on or opposition to programs such as public investment and national health insurance. If a multiracial political coalition were in place, it could pressure national public officials to consider seriously the interests of ordinary citizens when such issues are debated or up for adoption.

Furthermore, an organized political coalition poised to protect the interests of ordinary citizens would be in a position to join forces with other segments of society to generate political

support for programs that affect broader segments of population. For example, the creation of public infrastructure projects
to combat urban sprawl and ease the stresses of urban life would
benefit not only the low- to moderate-income groups, but the
more advantaged members of society as well.

In the final analysis, unless groups of ordinary citizens embrace the need for mutual political cooperation, they stand little
chance of generating the political muscle needed to ease their
economic and social burdens. Accordingly, broad public discussion of the merits of and need for a progressive multiracial political coalition is paramount. The extent of public support for
such a coalition will in large measure depend on the development and dissemination of political messages that resonate with
broad segments of the American citizenry. And the effectiveness
of the messages will rest in part upon how the issues to be addressed are defined.

The messages should convey the idea that changes in the
global economy have increased social inequality and created situations that enhance antagonisms between different racial groups,
and that although many of these groups are perceived as social
adversaries, they are potential allies in a reform coalition. Why?
Because they are all more or less vulnerable to impersonal global
economic changes.

However, given the racial friction that has adversely affected
intergroup relations, particularly in urban America, the formation of a multiracial reform coalition to pursue a mass-based economic agenda is likely to be difficult. Although it is important to
acknowledge the nation's racial divisions in order to meaningfully
address them, the constant attention they receive has obscured
the fact that black, white, Latino, Asian, and Native Americans

share many concerns, are beset by many similar problems, and
have many common values, aspirations, and norms.

People often assume that America's history of racial divisions
makes it unlikely that conditions of perceived interdependence
could be generated and lead to the development of a national
multiracial political coalition. Yet multiracial grassroots community organizations that exemplify conditions of perceived interdependence and have effectively mobilized different racial
groups do exist in the United States. The most notable are those
that represent the national community organization networks of
the Industrial Areas Foundation (IAF), especially the Texas Industrial Areas Foundation, which has created a model statewide
network of political influence.

IAF organizations clearly demonstrate that, despite America's
racial history, obstacles to sustained interracial cooperation can
be overcome by effective leadership. They therefore provide a
reference point for those who believe that the development of a
progressive national multiracial political coalition is desirable
and feasible. Although the IAF has been criticized for its rejection of explicitly race-specific issues, I think that this exclusion at
the local level can be a strength in multiracial coalition building
rather than a weakness. In forging a multiracial coalition, one
must take care to include issues that component groups find
meaningful while avoiding the issues those groups view as harmful to their interests. Affirmative action is seen by many blacks as
central to their ability to participate more fully in the benefits of
society; in contrast, many whites view affirmative action as a
threat because they fear it means rewarding unqualified persons
at the expense of the white middle class. How can a national mul-

tiracial coalition withstand such divergent interpretations of af-firmative action?

It is unlikely that resistance to quotas and numerical guide-lines can be overcome. But, as I showed in chapter 4, by refocus-ing the debate on *affirmative opportunity*, a case can be made for the types of inclusive policies that are supported by most white Americans and that are essential for the increased participation of black Americans in mainstream education and professional training.

Affirmative opportunity stresses the very American idea of equal opportunity: it offers job training, educational advance-ment, college scholarship, and job promotion based on indi-vidual effort, and it assesses achievement through flexible, merit-based criteria. The vocabulary of affirmative opportunity embraces many time-honored American ideals (achievement, effort, and persistence) and rejects the language appropriated by those who would claim that efforts to help the disadvantaged come at the expense of others in American society.

The rhetoric of affirmative opportunity will show that all Americans benefit from the widening of opportunity across all groups: increased levels of training and education will lead to the development of skilled workers who can enjoy the benefits of the new global workplace. Fully participating mothers and fathers will nurture children whose ability to replicate their parents' suc-cess will become firmer with each generation. Affirmative oppor-tunity, then, holds out the promise of a work-rewarding society for all Americans, and like the community improvement programs of the IAF organizations, it offers real solutions for minorities who have been handicapped by the cumulative effects of race.

Clearly, when all Americans have an avenue along which they may work to improve their lot, society as a whole benefits. This is, indeed, the idea of affirmative action. But the public debate over this concept has become unfairly mired in notions of quotas, preferential treatment, reverse discrimination, and artificially low standards. It is time, then, to change the vocabulary of our rhetoric and to speak and act in a manner that resonates with all groups.

On the basis of research on procedural fairness, we should expect strong public support for the idea of affirmative opportunity. Thus, even those who do not benefit directly from affirmative action appear willing to support a plan that reflects fairness. This is probably one of the reasons why opponents of affirmative action emphasize a term like *preferential treatment*, which implies behavior inconsistent with the idea of procedural fairness. Indeed, public opinion polls suggest that the defeat of the anti-affirmative action proposition in Houston, Texas, in 1997 was largely the result of the successful campaign by affirmative action proponents to exclude terms like *preferential treatment* from the proposition.

Although Americans are concerned about quotas and hiring, promoting, and admitting to college people who are "unqualified," they also believe in a level playing field. They therefore support the idea that equal opportunity programs are needed for minorities and women.

For all these reasons, leaders of a progressive multiracial coalition could include affirmative action programs as a part of the coalition's agenda and prevent it from becoming a divisive racial issue. They could first of all emphasize the idea of affirmative opportunity, as opposed to numerical guidelines or quotas.

They could also associate affirmative opportunity with the no-
tion of flexible, merit-based criteria of evaluation to enlarge the
pool of qualified candidates. In other words, they could implant
the idea of using flexible, merit-based criteria to identify candidates who have real merit or potential to succeed, not those who
are unqualified or lack the potential.

With the use of language such as affirmative opportunity, the
leaders of the coalition could also challenge many of the false assumptions concerning affirmative action, including assumptions
about preferential treatment so often emphasized by conservative critics. In short, by adopting and highlighting language that
embodies procedural fairness and equal opportunity, we increase
public support for affirmative action programs and thereby make
those programs acceptable as a vital part of a progressive multiracial coalition's agenda to reduce social inequality in the
American economy.

Closing the Book, Opening the Discussion

In this book I have worked to identify some of the real reasons
for the economic and social distress of the last three decades.
America's participation in global markets and the increasing
dominance of technology have introduced changes and challenges that are likely to continue apace. U.S. workers must be
better trained and more flexible than their industrial forebears.
The migration of people and workplaces from the city to the
suburbs has caused an urban sprawl that is ecologically burden-
some and expensive to maintain. Our poor, who are disproportionately America's minorities, have been isolated in growing
urban ghettos of despair and joblessness. And recent social,

monetary, fiscal, and trade policies have enhanced rather than al-
leviated social inequality.

And yet a sustained upward trend in the economy has improved conditions in the late 1990s. The lessening of the social
tensions that come with such an economic improvement allows
us room to discuss our country's future. In this book I have
demonstrated that the needs of ordinary, working Americans can
best be met by multiracial, broad-based coalitions. Although
elites invariably have a say in the leadership of the nation, the
voice of the people can be lessened by fragmenting the masses
into competing, divisive race-based groups. I call upon the
American people and especially the leaders of the poor, the
working classes, the displaced and the marginalized, the down-
sized and the deskilled, to set aside differences and work together
to discuss, in vocabularies that reject the unuseful particularisms
of race, the true task before us.

NOTES

Introduction

1. Richard B. Freeman, *The New Inequality: Creating Solutions for Poor America* (Boston: Beacon Press, 1999), 4.

2. Frank Levy, *The New Dollars and Dreams: American Incomes and Economic Change* (New York: Russell Sage, 1998), 2. However, Levy points out that from April 1997 to March 1998, hourly wages, adjusted for inflation, grew by a respectable 2 percent—although he cautions that "this growth occurred in a labor market that most people judge too tight to sustain" (2).

3. Ibid., 3.

4. Ibid., 4.

5. David Ellwood, "Winners and Losers in America: Taking the Measure of the New Economic Realities" (paper presented at the Aspen Domestic Strategy Group Meeting, Aspen, Colorado, July 1998).

6. Ernesto Cortes Jr., "What about Organizing?" in R. Freeman, 1999, 71–72.

7. Harold P. Freeman, "Poverty, Race, Racism, and Survival," *Annals of Epidemiology* 3, no. 2 (1993): 145–49; and Harold Freeman, "The

Meaning of Race in Science—Considerations for Cancer Research,"
Cancer 82, no. 1 (January 1, 1998): 219–25.

8. H. Freeman, 1993.

1. Racial Antagonisms and the
Expanding Ranks of the Have-Nots

1. Andrew Hacker, *Two Nations: Black and White, Separate, Hostile,
Unequal* (New York: Charles Scribner's Sons, 1992); and Douglas S.
Massey and Nancy Denton, *American Apartheid: Segregation and the
Making of the Underclass* (Cambridge: Harvard University Press, 1993).

2. Orlando Patterson, *The Ordeal of Integration: Progress and Resent-
ment in America's Racial Crisis* (Washington, D.C.: Civitas, 1997); and
Stephan Thernstrom and Abigail Thernstrom, *America in Black and
White* (New York: Simon and Schuster, 1997).

3. Lawrence Bobo and James R. Kluegel, "Opposition to Race Targeting: Self-Interest, Stratification Ideology, or Racial Attitudes?"
American Sociological Review 58 (1993): 443–64.

4. See, for example, a 1978 report by the National Urban League
entitled "The Illusion of Black Progress," which was prepared by
Robert Hill, the former research director of the National Urban
League, and included an introduction written by the then-president of
the National Urban League, John Jacobs. Robert B. Hill, *The Illusion of
Black Progress* (Washington, D.C.: National Urban League Research
Department, 1978).

5. For empirical support for the view that some whites were cynical
about government programs for blacks, see Stanley B. Greenberg,
Middle-Class Dreams: The Politics and Power of the New American Majority
(New York: Times Books, 1995); and Michelle Fine and Lois Weis, *The
Unknown City: Lives of Poor and Working-Class Young Adults* (Boston:
Beacon Press, 1998).

6. Greenberg, 1995.

7. Fine and Weis, 1998, 21.

8. This definition of racism is a modified version of one I have used before. See William Julius Wilson, *Power, Racism, and Privilege: Race Relations in Theoretical and Sociohistorical Perspectives* (New York: Macmillan, 1973).

9. Lawrence Bobo, James R. Kluegel, and Ryan A. Smith, "Laisse Faire Racism: The Crystallization of a Kinder, Gentler, Antiblack Ideology," in *Racial Attitudes in the 1990s*, ed. Steven A. Tuch and Jack K. Martin (Westport, Conn.: Praeger, 1997), 16–42.

10. Ibid.

11. Donald Noel, "Slavery and the Rise of Racism," in *The Origins of American Slavery and Racism*, ed. Donald Noel (Columbus, Ohio: Charles E. Merrill Publishers, 1972), 153–74.

12. Kenneth B. Clark, *Dark Ghetto: Dilemmas of Social Power* (New York: Harper and Row, 1965).

13. Ibid., 131.

14. Bobo, Kluegel, and Smith, 1997, 30.

15. Lawrence Bobo and James R. Kluegel, "Status, Ideology, and Dimensions of Whites' Racial Beliefs and Attitudes: Progress and Stagnation," in *Racial Attitudes in the 1990s*, ed. Steven A. Tuch and Jack K. Martin (Westport, Conn.: Praeger, 1997), 93–120. However, as noted by Jennifer Hochschild, in the same surveys "blacks also rank whites higher than the other three ethnicities on all six ratings. African Americans rank their own race most prone to accept welfare, more patriotic and work-oriented than Hispanics, and more intelligent and peaceful than both Asians and Hispanics" (*Facing Up to the American Dream: Race, Class, and the Soul of the Nation* [Princeton, N.J.: Princeton University Press, 1995], 111).

16. Lawrence Bobo and Ryan A. Smith, "Antipoverty Politics, Affirmative Action, and Racial Attitudes," in *Confronting Poverty: Prescriptions for Change*, ed. Sheldon H. Danziger, Gary D. Sandefur, and Daniel H. Weinberg, (Cambridge, Mass.: Harvard University Press, 1994), 365–95; and Benjamin Page and Robert Shapiro, *The Rational Public: Fifty Years of Trends in Americans' Policy Preferences* (Chicago: University of Chicago Press, 1992).

17. Bobo, Kluegel, and Smith, 1997, 25.

18. Bobo and Kluegel, 1997.

19. See Bobo, Kluegel, and Smith, 1997; and Bobo and Kluegel, 1997. My ideas about the new racial ideology have been greatly influenced by the work of Bobo and his colleagues.

20. James Kluegel, "Trends in Whites' Explanations of the Gap in Black-White Socioeconomic Status, 1977–1989," *American Sociological Review* 55 (1990): 512–25.

21. Bobo, Kluegel, and Smith, 1997.

22. Urie Bronfenbrenner, Stephen Ceci, Phyllis Moen, Peter Mc-Clelland, and Elaine Wethington, *The State of Americans: This Generation and the Next* (New York: The Free Press, 1996).

23. Alan B. Krueger, "What's Up with Wages?" (mimeo from the Industrial Relations Section, Princeton University, 1997).

24. Ibid., p. 3.

25. Jeff Faux, "You Are Not Alone," in *The New Majority*, ed. Stanley Greenberg and Theda Skocpol (New Haven: Yale University Press, 1997), 25.

26. Henry R. Richmond, *Program Design: The American Land Institute* (unpublished manuscript, 1997), 12.

27. Richard B. Freeman, *The New Inequality: Creating Solutions for Poor America* (Boston: Beacon Press, 1999), 8.

28. Krueger, 1997.

29. Ibid.

30. Sylvia Ann Hewlett and Cornel West, *The War against Parents* (New York: Houghton Mifflin, 1998).

31. Lawrence Mishel and Jared Bernstein, *The State of Working America, 1992–1993*, Economic Policy Institute Series (Armonk, N.Y.: M.E. Sharpe, 1993).

32. R. Freeman, 1999, 8–9.

33. Harris poll cited in Bronfenbrenner et al., 1996, 52.

34. Paul Krugman, "Superiority Complex," *New Republic*, November 3, 1997, p. 21.

35. Ibid.

36. Louis Uchitelle, "As Asia Stumbles, U.S. Stays in Ecomonic Stride," *New York Times*, December 7, 1997, p. 4.

37. Krueger, 1997.

38. Krugman, 1997, 22.

39. William Julius Wilson, *The Truly Disadvantaged: The Inner City, the Underclass, and Public Policy* (Chicago: University of Chicago Press, 1987); and "Taking Care of the Common Good: IAF Reflections on Work," draft no. 2, 2–09–95.

40. Faux, 1997, 25.

41. U.S. Department of Housing and Urban Development, *The State of the Cities* (Washington, D.C.: GPO, 1997), 40.

42. Paul Jargowsky, *Poverty and Place: Ghettos, Barrios, and the American City* (New York: Russell Sage Foundation, 1997).

43. Jargowsky, 1997, 35.

44. Paul Jargowsky, "Ghetto Poverty among Blacks in the 1980s," *Journal of Policy Analysis and Management* 13 (1994): 288–310.

45. Demetrios Caraley, "Washington Abandons the Cities," *Political Science Quarterly* 107 (spring 1992): 1–30.

46. U.S. Department of Housing and Urban Development.

47. Ibid.

48. Ibid.

49. Caraley, 1992.

50. R. Freeman, 1999, 7.

51. U. S. Bureau of the Census, *Current Population Reports*, series P-20, 1997.

52. Kristin Luker, *Dubious Conceptions: The Politics of Teenage Pregnancy* (Cambridge: Harvard University Press, 1996).

53. James K. Galbraith, *Created Unequal: The Crisis in American Pay* (New York: The Free Press, 1998), 12.

54. Stanley B. Greenberg, "Popularizing Progressive Politics," in *The New Majority*, ed. Stanley B. Greenberg and Theda Skocpol (New Haven: Yale University Press, 1997). Also see John Robinson

and Geoffrey Godbera, *Time for Life: The Surprising Ways Americans Use Their Time* (University Park, Pa.: Pennsylvania State University Press, 1997).

55. Ibid., 292.

2. Global Economic Changes and the Limits of the Race Relations Vision

1. Vivian Henderson, "Race, Economics, and Public Policy," *Crisis* 83 (fall 1975): 50–55.

2. Ray Marshall, "School-to-Work Processes in the United States" (paper presented at the Carnegie Corporation/Johann Jacobs Foundation, Marback Castle, Germany, November 3–5, 1995).

3. Alan Krueger, "Consequences of Computerization of the Workplace" (paper prepared for a conference entitled "Research, Technology and Employment," organized by the Spanish Presidency of the Council of the European Union, December 6–8, 1995).

4. Sylvia Nasar, "The Men in Prime of Life Spend Less Time Working," *New York Times*, December 1, 1994; and Stephen J. Rose, "On Shaky Ground: Rising Fears about Incomes and Earnings," Research Report No. 94–02 (October) (Washington, D.C.: National Commission for Employment Policy, 1994).

5. William Julius Wilson, *The Truly Disadvantaged: The Inner City, The Underclass, and Public Policy* (Chicago: University of Chicago Press, 1987); and William Julius Wilson, *When Work Disappears: The World of the New Urban Poor* (New York: Alfred A. Knopf, 1996).

6. John Bound and Harry Holzer, "Industrial Shifts, Skills Levels, and the Labor Market for White and Black Men," *Review of Economics and Statistics* 75 (August 1993): 387–96.

7. John Kasarda, "Industrial Restructuring and the Changing Location of Jobs," in *State of the Union: America in the 1990s*, vol. 1, ed. Reynolds Farley (New York: Russell Sage Foundation, 1995).

8. Maury B. Gittleman and David R. Howell, "Job Quality and Labor Market Segmentation in the 1980s: A New Perspective on the Effects of Employment Restructuring by Race and Gender," Working Paper no. 82 (Annandale-on-Hudson, N.Y.: Bard College, The Jerome Levy Economic Institute, March 1993). Henderson, 1975, 50–55.

9. Kasarda, 1995, 96.

10. Andrew Sum and Neal Fogg, "The Changing Economic Fortunes of Young Black Men in America," *The Black Scholar* (January, February, and March 1990): 47–55.

11. Ibid., 51.

12. Robert I. Lerman and Martin Rein, *Social Service Employment: An International Perspective* (New York: Russell Sage Foundation, forthcoming).

13. Ibid.

14. Alan B. Krueger, "How Computers Have Changed the Wage Structure: Evidence from Microdata, 1984–1989," *Quarterly Journal of Economics* (February 1993): 32–60.

15. Donna L. Hoffman and Thomas P. Novak, "Bridging the Racial Divide on the Internet," *Science*, April 17, 1998.

16. Reed Hundt, "The Information Superhighway: Ensuring that Poor and Minority Children Do Not Fall Further Behind" (paper presented at the Children's Defense Fund's Black Community Crusade for Children Working Committee Planning Retreat, Knoxville, Tenn., July 8, 1995).

17. Krueger, 1997; Lawrence Katz, "Wage Subsidies for the Disadvantaged," Working Paper 5679 (Cambridge, Mass.: National Bureau of Economic Research, Inc., 1996); and David Schwartzman, *Black Unemployment: Part of Unskilled Unemployment* (Westport, Conn.: Greenwood Press, 1997).

18. Schwartzman, 1997.

19. Ibid.

20. Galbraith, 1998, 9.

21. Krueger, 1997.

22. Schwartzman, 1997.

23. Richard B. Freeman and Lawrence F. Katz, "Rising Wage Inequality: The United States vs. Other Advanced Countries," in *Working Under Different Rules*, ed. Richard Freeman, 29–62 (New York: Russell Sage Foundation, 1994).

24. Ibid.

25. Sheldon H. Danziger and Peter Gottschalk, *America Unequal* (Cambridge: Harvard University Press, 1995).

26. Richmond, 1997.

27. Ibid., 10.

28. Krueger, 1997, 3.

29. Richmond, 1997.

30. Krueger, 1997, 8.

31. Ibid., 9.

32. U.S. Department of Housing and Urban Development, 1997.

33. Harry Holzer, *What Employers Want: Job Prospects for Less-Educated Workers* (New York: Russell Sage Foundation, 1995). Also see Center on Budget and Policy Priorities, "The Administration's $3 Billion Jobs Proposal" (Washington, D.C., GPO, 1966).

34. Sylvia Nasar, "Jobs Juggernaut Continues Surge: 300,000 Find Work," *New York Times*, March 7, 1998, pp. 1A and 14B.

35. A more detailed account of the transportation and networking problems of poor black workers is provided in William Julius Wilson, 1996.

36. Schwartzman, 1997.

37. Henderson, 1975, 54.

3. Building a Foundation for Multiracial Cooperation

1. Galbraith, 1998, 10.

2. Sheldon Danziger and Peter Gottschalk, introduction to *Uneven Tides: Rising Inequality in America*, ed. Sheldon Danziger and Peter Gottschalk (New York: Russell Sage Foundation, 1993).

3. Ibid., 15.

4. Edward M. Gramlich, Richard Kasten, and Frank Sammartino, "Growing Inequality in the 1980s: The Role of Federal Taxes and Cash Transfers," in *Uneven Tides: Rising Inequality in America*, ed. Sheldon Danziger and Peter Gottschalk (New York: Russell Sage Foundation, 1993), 245.

5. Schwartzman, 1997.

6. John M. Broder, "Party Spurned, Repays Clinton with Rebellion," *New York Times*, November 11, 1997, pp. A1 and A6.

7. Frank Borgers quoted in Steven Greenhouse, "Business and Labor Struggle with Globalization," *New York Times*, August 2, 1998.

8. David Sanger, "A Handicap for Clinton, but U.S. Still Dominates," *New York Times*, November 11, 1997, p. A6.

9. Galbraith, 1998, 8–9.

10. Ibid.

11. Faux, 1997, 32.

12. Ibid.

13. Ibid.

14. Ibid.

15. Richmond, 1997.

16. Ibid.

17. Ibid.

18. Jennifer Hochschild and Reuel Rogers, "Race Relations in a Diversifying Nation," in *New Directions: African Americans in a Diversifying Nation*, ed. James Jackson (forthcoming).

19. Raphael J. Sonenshein, "Biracial Coalitions in Big Cities: Why They Succeed, Why They Fail," in *Racial Politics in American Cities*, ed. Rufus P. Browing, Dale Rogers Marshall, and David H. Tabb (New York: Longman, 1990), 193–211.

20. For a good discussion and summary of this research, see D. W. Johnson, R. Johnson, and G. Maruyama, "Goal Interdependence and Interpersonal Attraction in Heterogeneous Classrooms: A Meta-Analysis," in *Groups in Contact: The Psychology of Desegregation*, ed. N.

Miller and M.B. Brewer, (Orlando, Fla.: Academic Press, 1984), 187–212. Also see Susan T. Fiske, "Stereotyping, Prejudice, and Discrimination," in *The Handbook of Social Psychology*, 4th ed., ed. D.T. Gilbert, S.T. Fiske, and G. Lindzey (New York: McGraw Hill, 1998).

21. Johnson, Johnson, and Maruyama, 1984.

22. Ibid., 199.

23. Ibid., 200.

24. Ibid., 202.

25. Marshall Ganz, private communication, October 16, 1998, Cambridge, Mass.

26. Sonenshein, 1990, 203.

27. John Brueggemann and Terry Boswell, "Realizing Solidarity: Sources of Interracial Unionism during the Great Depression," *Work and Occupations* 25 (November 1998): 437.

28. Ibid., 442.

29. Harry Kelber, "Start a 'Living Wage' Campaign," http://sweatmag .org/livstart.htm.

30. Other successful multiracial enterprises have been identified and described as promising practices by President Clinton's Initiative on Race. See "One America, Promising Practices: The President's Initiative on Race," http://www.whitehouse.gov/Initiatives/OneAmerica/ OneAmerica_ Links.html.

31. Ernesto Cortes Jr., "Reweaving the Social Fabric," *Boston Review* (June–September, 1994): 12–14.

32. Mark R. Warren, "Creating a Multi-Racial Democratic Community: Case Study of the Texas Industrial Areas Foundation" (paper prepared for the conference on Social Networks and Urban Poverty, Russell Sage Foundation, New York, New York, March 1–2, 1996).

33. See, for example, James Jennings, "The Politics of Black Empowerment in Urban America: Reflections on Race, Class and Community," in *Dilemmas of Activism*, ed. Joseph M. Kling and Prudence S. Posner (Philadelphia: Temple University Press, 1990).

34. Warren, 1996.

35. Ibid.

36. Cortes, 1994.

37. William Greider, *Who Will Tell the People: The Betrayal of American Democracy* (New York: Simon and Schuster, 1992), 235.

38. Peter Skerry, *Mexican Americans: An Ambivalent Minority* (New York: The Free Press, 1993), 157.

39. Warren, 1996.

40. Ibid.

41. Skerry, 1993, 157.

42. Ibid.

43. Warren, 1996.

44. Ibid.

45. Hochschild and Rogers, 6–7.

4. From "Racial Preference" to Affirmative Opportunity

1. Richard D. Kahlenberg, *Class, Race, and Affirmative Action* (New York: Basic Books, 1996).

2. Ibid.

3. Jerome Karabel, "No Alternative: The Effects of Color-Blind Admissions in California," in *Chilling Admissions: The Affirmative Action Crisis and the Search for Alternatives*, ed. Gary Orfield and Edward Miller (Cambridge Mass.: The Civil Rights Project, Harvard University, Harvard Education Publishing Group, 1998), 33–50; Thomas J. Kane, "Misconceptions in the Debate over Affirmative Action in College Admissions," in Orfield and Miller, *Chilling Admissions*, 17–32; and William G. Bowen and Derek Bok, *The Shape of the River: Long-Term Consequences of Considering Race in College and University Admissions* (Princeton, N.J.: Princeton University Press, 1998).

4. Karabel, 1998, 34.

5. Karabel, 1998, 38.

6. See, for example, the studies in Christopher Jencks and Meredith Phillips, eds., *The Black-White Test Score Gap* (Washington D.C.: Brookings Institution Press, 1998).

7. For two good discussions of the consequences of differential racial access to financial markets, see Dalton Conley, *Being Black, Living in Red: Race, Wealth, and Social Policy in America* (Berkeley: University of California Press, 1999); and Melvin Oliver and Tom Shapiro, *Black Wealth/White Wealth: A New Perspective on Racial Inequality* (New York: Routledge, 1995).

8. Jencks and Phillips, 1998.

9. Clause S. Fisher, Martin Jankowski, Sanchez Jankowski, Samuel R. Lucas, Ann Swidler, and Kim Voss, *Inequality and Design: Cracking the Bell Curve Myth* (Princeton: Princeton University Press, 1996); and Charles S. Tilly, *Durable Inequality* (Berkeley: University of California Press, 1998).

10. Nathan Glazer, "In Defense of Preference," *New Republic*, April 6, 1998, p. 24.

11. Ibid.

12. Karabel, 1998.

13. Ibid.

14. "California Sees Minority Admissions Rebound," *New York Times*, April 4, 1999, p. A18.

15. Susan Sturm and Lani Guinier, "The Future of Affirmative Action: Reclaiming the Innovative Ideal," *California Law Review* 84, no. 4 (July 1996): 953–1036.

16. Stephan Thernstrom and Abigail Thernstrom, *America in Black and White: One Nation Indivisible* (New York: Simon and Schuster, 1997).

17. Kane, 1998, 19.

18. Sturm and Guinier, 1996, 957.

19. For a discussion of the studies that show a weak relationship between standard aptitude test scores and job performance, see ibid.

20. Michael Selmi, "Testing for Equality: Merit, Efficiency, and the Affirmative Action Debate," *UCLA Law Review* 42 (1995): 1252–77.

21. Lani Guinier, Michelle Fine, and Jane Balin, "Becoming Gentlemen: Women's Experiences at One Ivy League Law School," *University of Pennsylvania Law Review* 143 (1994); and Sturm and Guinier, 1996. Sturm and Guinier present findings on the correlation between LSAT scores and the first-year grade point averages of white students at the University of Texas, as reported in the Declaration of Martin M. Shapiro at 15, *Hopwood v. Texas*, 861 F. Supp. 551 (W.D. Tex. 1994), (No. A-92-CAA-563-SS).

22. My views on affirmative action in the remainder of this chapter have benefited greatly from discussions with Noel Salinger of the Irving B. Harris School of Public Policy at the University of Chicago. Salinger helped me draft several memoranda on affirmative action for the White House, and my views were first developed in those memoranda.

23. Sturm and Guinier, 1996, 1020.

24. For a good discussion of the research on the comparative relationships between the SAT and college freshmen grades and high school grades and college freshmen grades, see ibid.

25. Mark Kelman, "Concepts of Discrimination in 'General Ability' Job Testing," *Harvard Law Review* 104 (1991): 1158, 1159; and ibid.

26. Sturm and Guinier, 1996, 988.

27. Ibid.

28. Frances A. McMorris, "Test-Prep Fees Deter Black Law Applicants," *Wall Street Journal*, March 23, 1988, pp. B1–B5.

29. Ibid.

30. Sturm and Guinier, 1996, 991.

31. Susan Wilbur and Marguerite Bonous-Hammarth, "Testing a New Approach to Admissions: The Irvine Experience," in Orfield and Miller, *Chilling Admissions*, 111.

32. Ibid., 113.

33. Ibid.

34. Ibid.

35. Ibid., 116.

36. Sturm and Guinier, 1996.

37. "Statement of Dean Jeffrey S. Lehman of the University of Michigan Law School," Ann Arbor, Michigan, 1977.

38. *Report and Recommendations of the Admissions Committee*, University of Michigan Law School, Ann Arbor, Michigan, April 22, 1992, pp. 7 and 11–12.

39. This statement is based on personal observation and interaction with the black law students at the University of Michigan, as well as on conversations with Jeffrey S. Lehman, dean of the University of Michigan Law School.

40. Glazer, 1998, 19.

41. Lawrence Bobo, "Race, Interests, and Beliefs about Affirmative Action," *American Behavioral Scientist* 41, no. 7 (1998): 986. Also see Charlotte Steeh and Maria Krysan, "Poll Trends: Affirmative Action and the Public," *Public Opinion Quarterly* 60: 128–58.

42. Lawrence Bobo and Ryan A. Smith, "Antipoverty Politics, Affirmative Action, and Racial Attitudes," in *Confronting Poverty: Prescriptions for Change*, ed. Sheldon H. Danziger, Gary D. Sandefur, and Daniel H. Weinberg (Cambridge: Harvard University Press, 1994), 365–95.

43. Barry Bluestone and Mary Huff Stevenson, *Greater Boston in Transition: Race and Ethnicity in a Renaissance Region* (New York: Russell Sage, forthcoming 1999).

44. Lawrence Bobo and James R. Kluegel, "Opposition to Race Targeting: Self-Interest, Stratification Ideology, or Racial Attitudes?" *American Sociological Review* 58 (1993): 446.

45. Swain, 1998.

46. David A. Kravitz and Judith Platania, "Attitudes and Beliefs about Affirmative Action: Effects of Target and of Respondent Sex and Ethnicity," *Journal of Applied Psychology* 78, no. 6: 928–38.

47. J.H. Lea, H. Smith, and T.R. Tyler, "Predicting Support for Compensatory Public Policies: Who, Why, and Now" (unpublished manuscript, University of California, Berkeley, 1995).

48. Swain, 1998.

49. Karabel, 1998, 22.

50. Ibid.

51. Sturm and Guinier, 1996, 956.

5. Bridging the Racial Divide and Coalition Politics

1. Richard Parker, "Centrism, Populist Style," *The Nation*, October 7, 1996, p. 20.

BIBLIOGRAPHY

Anyon, Jean. 1997. *Ghetto Schooling: A Political Economy of Urban Educational Reform.* New York: Teachers College Press.

Blau, Francine D., Marianne A. Ferber, and Anne E. Winkler. 1998. *The Economics of Women, Men, and Work.* 3d ed. Upper Saddle River, N.J.: Prentice Hall.

Bluestone, Barry, and Stephen Rose. 1998. "The Unmeasured Labor Force: The Growth in Work Hours." Public Policy Brief No. 39. The Jerome Levy Economic Institute of Bard College, Annandale-on-Hudson, New York.

Bluestone, Barry, and Mary Huff Stevenson. 1999 (forthcoming). *Greater Boston in Transition: Race and Ethnicity in a Renaissance Region.* New York: Russell Sage Foundation.

Bobo, Lawrence. 1998. "Race, Interests, and Beliefs about Affirmative Action." *American Behavioral Scientist* 41, no. 7: 986.

Bobo, Lawrence, and James R. Kluegel. 1993. "Opposition to Race Targeting: Self-Interest, Self-Stratification Ideology, or Racial Attitudes?" *American Sociological Review* 58: 443–64.

———. 1997. "Status, Ideology, and Dimensions of Whites' Racial Beliefs and Attitudes: Progress and Stagnation." In *Racial Attitudes in the 1990s.* Ed. Steven A. Tuch and Jack K. Martin. Westport, Conn.: Praeger.

Bobo, Lawrence, James R. Kluegel, and Ryan A. Smith. 1997. "Laisse Faire Racism: The Crystallization of a Kinder, Gentler, Antiblack Ideology." In *Racial Attitudes in the 1990s.* Ed. Steven A. Tuch and Jack K. Martin. Westport, Conn.: Praeger.

Bobo, Lawrence, and Ryan A. Smith. 1994. "Antipoverty Politics, Affirmative Action, and Racial Attitudes." In *Confronting Poverty: Prescriptions for Change.* Ed. Sheldon H. Danziger, Gary D. Sandefur, and Daniel H. Weinberg. Cambridge, Mass.: Harvard University Press.

Bound, John, and Harry Holzer. 1993. "Industrial Shifts, Skills Levels, and the Labor Market for White and Black Men." *Review of Economic and Statistics* 75 (August): 387–96.

Bowen, William G., and Derek Bok. 1998. *The Shape of the River: Long-Term Consequences of Considering Race in College and University Admissions.* Princeton, N.J.: Princeton University Press.

Broder, John M. 1997. "Party Spurned, Repays Clinton with Rebellion." *New York Times,* November 11, pp. A1, A6.

Bronfenbrenner, Urie, Stephen Ceci, Phyllis Moen, Peter McClelland, and Elaine Wethington. 1996. *The State of Americans: This Generation and the Next.* New York: The Free Press.

Brueggemann, John, and Terry Boswell. 1998. "Realizing Solidarity: Sources of Interracial Unionism during the Great Depression." *Work and Occupations* 25 (November): 436–481.

Caraley, Demetrios. 1992. "Washington Abandons the Cities." *Political Science Quarterly* (spring) 107: 1–30.

Card, David, and Thomas Lemieux. 1994. "Changing Wage Structure and Black-White Differentials among Men and Women: A Longitudinal Analysis." *Working Paper Series,* Working Paper no. 4755. Cambridge, Mass.: National Bureau of Economic Research, May.

Center on Budget and Policy Priorities. 1996. *The Administration's $3 Billion Jobs Proposal.* Washington, D.C.

Clark, Kenneth B. 1965. *Dark Ghetto: Dilemmas of Social Power.* New York: Harper and Row.

Conley, Dalton. 1999. *Being Black, Living in Red: Race, Wealth, and Social Policy in America.* Berkeley: University of California Press.

Cortes, Ernesto Jr. 1994. "Reweaving the Social Fabric." *Boston Review* (June–September): 12–14.

———. 1999. "What about Organizing?" In *The New Inequality: Creating Solutions for Poor America*, Richard B. Freeman. Boston: Beacon Press.

Danziger, Sheldon, and Peter Gottschalk. 1993. Introduction to *Uneven Tides: Rising Inequality in America.* Ed. Sheldon Danziger and Peter Gottschalk. New York: Russell Sage Foundation.

———. 1995. *America Unequal.* Cambridge: Harvard University Press.

Ellwood, David. 1998. "Winners and Losers in America: Taking Measure of the New Economic Realities." Paper presented at the Aspen Domestic Strategy Group Meeting, Aspen, Colorado, July.

Faux, Jeff. 1997. "You Are Not Alone." In *The New Majority.* Ed. Stanley Greenberg and Theda Skocpol. New Haven: Yale University Press.

Fine, Michelle, and Lois Weis. 1998. *The Unknown City: Lives of Poor and Working-Class Young Adults.* Boston: Beacon Press.

Fisher, Clause S., Martin Jankowski, Sanchez Jankowski, Samuel R. Lucas, Ann Swindler, and Kim Voss. 1996. *Inequality and Design: Cracking the Bell Curve Myth.* Princeton: Princeton University Press.

Fiske, Susan T. 1998. "Stereotyping, Prejudice, and Discrimination." In *The Handbook of Social Psychology.* 3d ed. Ed. D. T. Gilbert, S. T. Fiske, and G. Lindzey. New York: McGraw Hill.

Freeman, Harold P. 1993. "Poverty, Race, Racism, and Survival." *Annals of Epidemiology* 3, no. 2 (1993): 145–49.

———. 1998. "The Meaning of Race in Science—Considerations for Cancer Research." *Cancer* 82, no. 1 (January): 219–25.

Freeman, Richard B. 1999. *The New Inequality: Creating Solutions for Poor America.* Boston: Beacon Press.

Freeman, Richard B., and Lawrence Katz. 1994. "Rising Wage Inequality: The United States vs. Other Advanced Countries." In *Working under Different Rules*. Ed. Richard B. Freeman, 29–62. New York: Russell Sage Foundation.

Galbraith, James K. 1998. *Created Unequal: The Crisis in American Pay*. New York: The Free Press.

Gittleman, Maury B., and David R. Howell. 1993. "Job Quality and Labor Market Segmentation in the 1980s: A New Perspective on the Effects of Employment Restructuring by Race and Gender." Working Paper No. 82 (March), The Jerome Levy Economic Institute of Bard College, Annandale-on-Hudson, New York.

Glazer, Nathan. 1998. "In Defense of Preference." *The New Republic*, April 6.

Gramlich, Edward M., Richard Kasten, and Frank Sammartino. 1993. "Growing Inequality in the 1980s: The Role of Federal Taxes and Cash Transfers." In *Uneven Tides: Rising Inequality in America*. Ed. Sheldon Danziger and Peter Gottschalk, 225–49. New York: Russell Sage Foundation.

Greenberg, Stanley B. 1995. *Middle-Class Dreams: The Politics and Power of the New American Majority*. New York: Times Books.

———. 1997. "Popularizing Progressive Politics." In *The New Majority*. Ed. Stanley B. Greenberg and Theda Skocpol. New Haven: Yale University Press.

Greenhouse, Steven. 1998. "Business and Labor Struggle with Globalization." *New York Times*, August 2.

Greider, William. 1992. *Who Will Tell the People: The Betrayal of American Democracy*. New York: Simon and Schuster.

Guinier, Lani, Michelle Fine, and Jane Balin. 1994. "Becoming Gentlemen: Women's Experiences at One Ivy League Law School." *University of Pennsylvania Law Review* 143.

Guinier, Lani, and Gerald Torres. 1999. "Critical Race Theory Revisited." The second of three Nathan I. Huggins Lectures, Harvard University, Cambridge, Massachusetts, April 20.

Hacker, Andrew. 1992. *Two Nations: Black and White, Separate, Hostile, Unequal*. New York: Charles Scribner's Sons.

Hamilton, Dona Cooper, and Charles V. Hamilton. 1997. *Race and Social Welfare Policies of Civil Rights Organizations*. New York: Columbia University Press.

Henderson, Vivian. 1975. "Race, Economics, and Public Policy." *Crisis* 83 (fall): 50–55.

Hewlett, Sylvia Ann, and Cornel West. 1998. *The War against Parents*. New York: Houghton Mifflin.

Hill, Robert B. 1978. *The Illusion of Black Progress*. Washington, D.C.: The National Urban League Research Department.

Hochschild, Jennifer L. 1995. *Facing Up to the American Dream: Race, Class, and the Soul of the Nation*. Princeton, N.J.: Princeton University Press.

———. 1999. "The Strange Career of Affirmative Action." *Ohio State Law Journal* 59 (winter): 997–1037.

Hochschild, Jennifer L., and Reuel Rogers. Forthcoming. "Race Relations in a Diversifying Nation." In *New Directions: African Americans in a Diversifying Nation*. Ed. James Jackson.

Hoffman, Donna L., and Thomas P. Novak. 1998. "Bridging the Racial Divide on the Internet." *Science* (April 17): 219–25.

Holzer, Harry. 1995. *What Employers Want: Job Prospects for Less-Educated Workers*. New York: Russell Sage Foundation.

Hundt, Reed. 1995. "The Information Superhighway: Ensuring that Poor and Minority Children Do Not Fall Further Behind." Paper presented at the Children's Defense Fund's Black Community Crusade for Children Working Committee Planning Retreat, Knoxville, Tenn., July 8.

Jahoda, Marie, Paul F. Lazarsfeld, and Hans Zeisel. 1971. *The Sociography of an Unemployed Community*. Chicago: Aldine-Atherton.

Jargowsky, Paul. 1994. "Ghetto Poverty among Blacks in the 1980s." *Journal of Policy Analysis and Management* 13: 288–310.

———. 1997. *Poverty and Place: Ghettos, Barrios, and the American City*. New York: Russell Sage Foundation.

Jencks, Christopher, and Meredith Phillips, eds. 1998. *The Black-White Test Score Gap*. Washington, D.C.: Brookings Institution Press.

Jennings, James. 1990. "The Politics of Black Empowerment in Urban America: Reflections on Race, Class and Community." In *Dilemmas of Activism*. Ed. Joseph M. Kling and Prudence S. Posner. Philadelphia: Temple University Press.

Johnson, D.W., R. Johnson, and G. Maruyama. 1984. "Goal Interdependence and Interpersonal Attraction in Heterogeneous Classrooms: A Meta-Analysis." In *Groups in Contact: The Psychology of Desegregation*, ed. N. Miller and M.B. Brewer. Orlando, Fla.: Academic Press.

Juhn, Chinhui, Kevin M. Murphy, and Brooks Pierce. 1991. "Accounting for the Slowdown in Black-White Convergence." In *Workers and Their Wages: Changing Patterns in the United States*. Ed. Marvin H. Kosters. Washington, D.C.: American Enterprise Institute Press.

Kahlenberg, Richard D. 1996. *Class, Race, and Affirmative Action*. New York: Basic Books.

Kane, Thomas J. 1998. "Misconceptions in the Debate over Affirmative Action in College Admissions." In *Chilling Admissions: The Affirmative Action Crisis and the Search for Alternatives*. Ed. Gary Orfield and Edward Miller, 17–32. Cambridge, Mass.: Harvard Education Publishing Group, The Civil Rights Project, Harvard University.

Karabel, Jerome. 1998. "No Alternative: The Effects of Color-Blind Admissions in California." In *Chilling Admissions: The Affirmative Action Crisis and the Search for Alternatives*. Ed. Gary Orfield and Edward Miller, 33–50. Cambridge, Mass.: Harvard Education Publishing Group, The Civil Rights Project, Harvard University.

Kasarda, John. 1995. "Industrial Restructuring and the Changing Location of Jobs." In *State of the Union: America in the 1990s*. Vol. 1. Ed. Reynolds Farley. New York: Russell Sage Foundation.

Katz, Lawrence. 1996. "Wage Subsidies for the Disadvantaged." Working Paper 5679. Cambridge, Mass.: National Bureau of Economic Research.

Kelman, Mark. 1991. "Concepts of Discrimination in 'General Ability' Job Testing." *Harvard Law Review* 104: 1158, 1159.

Kluegel, James R. 1990. "Trends in Whites' Explanations of the Gap in Black-White Socioeconomic Status, 1977–1989." *American Sociological Review* 55: 512–25.

Kluegel, James R., and Ryan A. Smith. 1983. "Affirmative Action Attitudes: Effects of Self-Interest, Racial Affect, and Stratification Beliefs on Whites' Views." *Social Forces* 61: 797–824.

Kravitz, David A., and Judith Platania. 1993. "Attitudes and Beliefs about Affirmative Action: Effects of Target and of Respondent Sex and Ethnicity." *Journal of Applied Psychology* 78, no. 6: 928–38.

Krueger, Alan. 1993. "How Computers Have Changed the Wage Structure: Evidence from Microdata, 1984–1989." *Quarterly Journal of Economics* (February): 32–60.

———. 1995. "Consequences of Computerization of the Workplace." Paper prepared for conference entitled "Research, Technology and Employment." Organized by the Spanish Presidency of the Council of the European Union, December 6–8.

———. 1997. "What's Up with Wages?" Mimeo from the Industrial Relations Section, Princeton University.

———. 1999. "Measuring Labor's Share." Working Paper no. 413, Industrial Relations Section, Princeton University, January.

Krugman, Paul. 1997. "Superiority Complex." *New Republic*, November 3.

Lea, J.H., H. Smith, and T.R. Tyler. 1995. "Predicting Support for Compensatory Public Policies: Who, Why, and Now." Unpublished manuscript, Berkeley: University of California.

Lerman, Robert I., and Martin Rein. Forthcoming. *Social Service Employment: An International Perspective*. New York: Russell Sage Foundation.

Levy, Frank. 1998. *The New Dollars and Dreams: American Incomes and Economic Change*. New York: Russell Sage Foundation.

Loury, Glenn C. 1996. "Absolute California: Can the Golden State Go Color-Blind?" *The New Republic*, November 18, pp. 17–20.

———. 1997. "How to Mend Affirmative Action." *The Public Interest* (spring): 33–43.

Luker, Kristin. 1996. *Dubious Conceptions: The Politics of Teenage Pregnancy*. Cambridge: Harvard University Press.

Marshall, Ray. 1994. "School-to-Work Processes in the United States." Paper presented at the Carnegie Corporation/Johann Jacobs Foundation, Marbach Castle, Germany, November 3–5.

Massey, Douglas S., and Nancy Denton. 1993. *American Apartheid: Segregation and the Making of the Underclass*. Cambridge: Harvard University Press.

McMorris, Frances A. 1988. "Test-Prep Fees Deter Black Law Applicants." *Wall Street Journal*, March 23, pp. B1–B5.

Mishel, Lawrence, and Jared Bernstein. 1993. *The State of Working America, 1992–1993*. Economic Institute Series. Armonk, N.Y.: M.E. Sharpe.

———. 1994. *The State of Working America, 1994–1995*. Armonk, N.Y.: M.E. Sharpe.

Nasar, Sylvia. 1994. "The Men in Prime of Life Spend Less Time Working." *New York Times*, December 1.

———. 1998. "Jobs Juggernaut Continues Surge: 300,000 Find Work." *New York Times*, March 7, pp. 1A and 14B.

Noel, Donald. 1972. "Slavery and the Rise of Racism." In *The Origins of American Slavery and Racism*. Ed. Donald Noel. Columbus, Ohio: Charles E. Merrill Publishers.

Oliver, Melvin, and Tom Shapiro. 1995. *Black Wealth/White Wealth: A New Perspective on Racial Inequality*. New York: Routledge.

Page, Benjamin I., and Robert Y. Shapiro. 1992. *The Rational Public: Fifty Years of Trends in Americans' Policy Preferences*. Chicago: University of Chicago Press.

Parker, Richard. 1996. "Centrism, Populist Style." *The Nation*, October 7, pp. 19–21.

Patterson, Orlando. 1997. *The Ordeal of Integration: Progress and Resentment in America's Racial Crisis*. Washington, D.C.: Civitas.

Report and Recommendations of the Admissions Committee. 1992. Ann Arbor, Mich.: University of Michigan Law School, April 22.

Richmond, Henry R. 1997. *Program Design: The American Land Institute*. Unpublished manuscript.

Robinson, John P., and Geoffrey Godbera. 1997. *Time for Life: The Surprising Ways Americans Use Their Time*. University Park, Pa.: Pennsylvania State University Press.

Rose, Stephen J. 1994. "On Shaky Ground: Rising Fears about Incomes and Earnings." Research Report No. 94–02 (October). Washington, D.C.: National Commission for Employment Policy.

Sanger, David. 1997. "A Handicap for Clinton, but U.S. Still Dominates." *New York Times*, November 11.

Schor, Juliet. 1992. *The Overworked American: The Unexpected Decline of Leisure*. New York: Basic Books.

Schwartzman, David. 1997. *Black Unemployment: Part of Unskilled Unemployment*. Westport, Conn.: Greenwood Press.

Selmi, Michael. 1995. "Testing for Equality: Merit, Efficiency, and the Affirmative Action Debate," *UCLA Law Review* 42: 1252–77.

Skerry, Peter. 1993. *Mexican Americans: An Ambivalent Minority*. New York: The Free Press.

Sonenshein, Raphael J. 1990. "Biracial Coalitions in Big Cities: Why They Succeed, Why They Fail." In *Racial Politics in American Cities*. Ed. Rufus P. Browing, Dale Rogers Marshall, and David H. Tabb. New York: Longman.

"Statement of Dean Jeffrey S. Lehman of the University of Michigan Law School." 1977. Mimeo. Ann Arbor, Michigan.

Steeh, Charlotte, and Maria Krysan. 1996. "Poll Trends: Affirmative Action and the Public, 1970–1995." *Public Opinion Quarterly* 60: 128–58.

Sturm, Susan, and Lani Guinier. 1996. "The Future of Affirmative Action: Reclaiming the Innovative Ideal." *California Law Review* 84, no. 4 (July): 953–1036.

Sum, Andrew, and Neal Fogg. 1990. "The Changing Economic Fortunes of Young Black Men in America." *The Black Scholar* (January, February, and March): 47–55.

Swain, Carol M. 1998. "Affirmative Action: A Search for Consensus." Paper presented at the National Academy of Sciences, Research Conference on Racial Trends in the United States, Washington, D.C., October 15.

"Taking Care of the Common Good: IAF Reflections on Work." Draft No. 2, 2–09–95.

Thernstrom, Stephan, and Abigail Thernstrom. 1997. *America in Black and White*. New York: Simon and Schuster.

Tilly, Charles S. 1998. *Durable Inequality*. Berkeley: University of California Press.

Tyler, Tom R. 1997. "Procedural Fairness and Compliance with the Law." *Swiss Journal of Economics and Statistics* 133: 219–40.

Uchitelle, Louis. 1997. "As Asia Stumbles, U.S. Stays in Economic Stride." *New York Times*, December 7.

U.S. Bureau of the Census. 1997. *Current Population Reports*. Series P-20. Washington, D.C.: GPO.

U.S. Department of Housing and Urban Development. 1997. *The State of the Cities*. Washington, D.C.: GPO.

Warren, Mark R. 1996. "Creating a Multi-Racial Democratic Community: Case Study of the Texas Industrial Areas Foundation." Prepared for the conference on Social Networks and Urban Poverty, Russell Sage Foundation, New York, New York, March 1–2.

Wilbur, Susan, and Marguerite Bonous-Hammarth. 1998. "Testing a New Approach to Admissions: The Irvine Experience." In *Chilling Admissions: The Affirmative Action Crisis and the Search for Alternatives*. Ed. Gary Orfield and Edward Miller, 111–22. Cambridge Mass.: Harvard Education Publishing Group, The Civil Rights Project, Harvard University.

Williamson, Thad. 1997. "True Prophecy? A Critical Examination of the Sociopolitical Stance of the Mainline Protestant Churches." *Union Seminary Quarterly Review* 51, nos. 1–2: 79–115.

Wilson, William Julius. 1973. *Power, Racism, and Privilege: Race Relations in Theoretical and Sociohistorical Perspectives.* New York: Macmillan Co.

———. 1987. *The Truly Disadvantaged: The Inner City, the Underclass, and Public Policy.* Chicago: University of Chicago Press.

———. 1996. *When Work Disappears: The World of the New Urban Poor.* New York: Alfred A. Knopf.

INDEX

affirmative action, 8, 12, 23,
92–110; affirmative opportunity,
8, 111–16, 125–27 (flexible,
merit-based criteria and, 112,
127; and multiracial political
coalition, 115–16); class-based,
95–99; flexible, merit-based criteria and, 102–8; opposition to,
11, 21, 39, 109, 124–26
affirmative opportunity. *See* affirmative action
African Americans, 7, 11–22, 38,
77, 112, 113, 115, 117, 121–23,
125; core values of, 78; and cultural deprivation theories,
16–18; and flexible admissions
criteria, 106; in free trade debate, 72; in high-poverty metropolitan neighborhoods, 35;
home computer ownership
among, 51–52; in IAF, 86, 87,
89–92; impact of global economic forces on, 43, 45–46, 54,
63–66; during Jim Crow segregation era, 15–16; lone-parent
families of, 41; and shifts in
labor demand, 47–50, 59–63;
social programs for, 13, 20, 110;
standardized test scores of,
97–100, 102, 104; stereotyping
of, 19, 21; wage declines for, 39
Albany (New York), living wage
campaign in, 84
Alinsky, Saul, 85
American Civil Rights Coalition, 109n
Anyon, Jean, 18n
Asian Americans, 11, 13, 77, 117,
123; and racial stereotypes, 19;
standardized test scores of, 104
Atlanta, shifts in labor demand
in, 60

balanced budget, 80
Baltimore: ghetto census tracts in,
36; living wage campaign in, 84

157

Indexer: Ruth Elwell
Compositor: Impressions Book and Journal Services, Inc.
Text: 10/15 Janson
Display: Akzidenz Grotesk
Printer and binder: Haddon Craftsmen, Inc.